HIGH FASHION
KNITTING FOR DOLLS

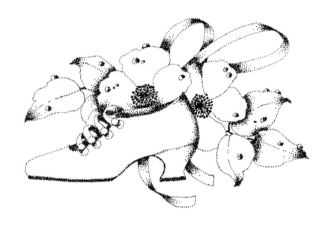

HIGH FASHION KNITTING FOR DOLLS

Furze Hewitt

Photography by Robert Roach
Line illustrations by Josephine Hoggan

Kangaroo Press

To my grandchildren
and their parents

Acknowledgments

My grateful thanks to Robert Roach for his exceptional skill as a photographer of white lace knitting, and his artistic skill in helping create the sets.

A special thankyou to the following: The Knitters: Edna Lomas, Thea Moore, Kathy Grin and Joan Eckersley. The doll creators: Patricia Blyth, Ria Warke, Ellen Watt, Aileen Sellen and Jan Clements. James Botham for lending his antiques. Carol Davey of Dunbar Cottage Gallery for the use of her extensive collection of textiles and paraphernalia. John Cummins of Queanbeyan Books and Prints, still searching for knitting patterns. Josephine M. Hoggan for her delightful drawings. Thea Moore, a second thankyou for her advice and sewing skills. Dina Tagliapietra for typing the manuscript and Rina Tagliapietra for all her help.

The following have helped in various ways: Carol Coates, Maurine Rogers, Patsy Ranger, Roslyn Panetta, Ann Dalton, Paddy Lloyd, Patricia Wain, Anna Sliwinski, Glyn Hopson, Lara Blyth, Isabel Bunting, Flick Evans, Barry Gilmour, Wendy Loftus, Pamela Ball, Norma Treloar, Vicki Hersey, Billie Daley, Val Cooper, Michael Roath and Anne Savage.

My thanks to everyone who made this book possible.

Technical note

All the photographs in this book were taken using:

- Kodak Ektachrome *Plus*, Professional, 35 mm Daylight Slide Film, processed by Kodak.

- Zeiss Ikon/Voigtländer ICAREX 35S camera with Carl Zeiss ULTRON 50 mm, f1.8 lens (bought in 1970).

© *Furze Hewitt 1993*

First published in 1993 by Kangaroo Press Pty Ltd
3 Whitehall Road Kenthurst NSW 2156 Australia
P.O. Box 6125 Dural Delivery Centre NSW 2158 Australia
Typeset by G.T. Setters Pty Limited
Printed in Hong Kong through Colorcraft Ltd

ISBN 0 86417 557 4

Contents

Zena (page 80) presenting the ribbon to the Merry Maiden (page 88).

Foreword

It is a well-known fact that the art of knitting, which requires the minimum amount of equipment, is a relaxing one. Under the guidance of an expert it becomes even more so.

Furze Hewitt was already an established writer of knitting books when she turned her attention to knitting for dolls. Her first book in this category, *Heirloom Knitting for Dolls*, published last year, has established her reputation with dollmakers as a person who knows her craft and who also knows how to pass on her information in a clear, concise and easy-to-follow form.

This new volume can do nothing but enhance that well-deserved reputation and will be a valuable addition, not only to dollmakers' libraries but also to those of the many enthusiasts who follow the art for its own sake.

Furze has delved into the dim and distant past to rediscover patterns which could have been lost forever but are now included in a wonderful array of outfits, not only for antique treasures but also for the more modern dolls. I am sure mothers, aunts and grandmothers will enjoy re-creating these designs which may well be the family heirlooms of the future.

For the non-knitter Furze provides a wealth of great photography of antique and modern dolls and accessories.

Pat Blyth, Master Dollmaker

Girls in white dresses performing the maypole dance.

Introduction

This book of knitting for dolls is intended as an alternative to dressmaking. The designs have an old world charm, and the patterns are simple and effective.

Dolls' bodies vary in size and shape, so approximate estimates of yarn requirements are given. The estimates are generous; if in doubt, purchase an extra ball of yarn. A useful chart compiled and supplied by Amies Tricote has been included on page 16 to assist you in finding an alternative yarn or ply, should you desire.

A brief note on the designs presented here

I was fortunate to obtain from Ormond Antiques (*see* Suppliers) the exquisite antique French hats the dolls are wearing. These hats and the appealing dolls lent by Pat Blyth, of Blithe Bébés (*see* Doll Studios) inspired my creations.

Using exclusive yarns in subtle colours, the simple designs, worn with aplomb, evoke an Edwardian air.

The patterns for the white gowns are from the nineteenth century, and were skilfully knitted by Edna Lomas. Edna also made the miniature tablecloth, and the shawl from the same design. The circular cloth and shawl are knitted on two needles. Those of you who prefer two-needle knitting will appreciate this design.

A variety of dolls appear in the book, including antique and reproduction porcelain, antique and modern peg, carved, knitted and vinyl dolls. All wear knitted garments. Ria Warke (*see* Doll Studios) crafted Ringer, The Dollmaker, and his wife Lucy, The Knitter. Ellen Watt (*see* Doll Studios) created the grandmother holding the antique baby doll. Kathy Grin designed and knitted Bridget especially for this book.

Thea Moore made the uniform for Gunson the Sailor. The pattern for his outfit came from an old nineteenth century publication. Thea also made, from her own designs, the ensemble on the baby doll, the fluted bedcover, and Elizabeth and her clothes.

The Mountain Ash Bed created by Flick Evans was made to a scale of 1 to 5½. Of simple colonial design, it is dressed in 4-ply cotton, the heavier yarn enhancing the rustic charm of early Australian furniture. The valance—Turkish Delight (page 53)—is an effective design. The pattern dates from the 1840s, the same period as the original colonial bed.

The exquisite collars, Capricornia and Rosamunda (on pages 39 and 40), were created for the book by Kathie Savage of Berwick, Victoria (*see* Doll Studios). The coathangers and lavender bags on page 72 are Joan Eckersley designs, also made for this book. These tiny items would make a delightful gift for a doll lover.

Included in the book are a selection of laces and trims, sack socks, mittens, bonnets and underwear.

Many of the patterns came from nineteenth century periodicals, others from generous knitters. The designs were knitted in cotton, which is durable, easily laundered, readily available, comparatively inexpensive, and ideal for dolls' fashion. Also, the use of designer yarns enhances the garments with subtle dyes not available in inferior or synthetic threads.

Knitting your doll's outfit works out at a fraction of the cost of a material gown. Keep a look out for yarn sales and don't be put off by discarded murky shades. These are the colours favoured in the nineteenth century, and I have used some of these unusual colours in the book. When you have completed the outfit, don't spoil it with cheap buttons and inferior trims.

We hope you enjoy the book we have created, and that the designs inspire you to knit for your doll.

Happy knitting!

Lucy the Knitter working on a length of Victorian eyelet lace (page 97).

Abbreviations and Terms

Abbreviations are used in knitting instructions to save space, and to make the pattern easier to follow. It is important to read, and understand, the abbreviations before beginning to knit a pattern.

In this book most of the patterns use standard British abbreviations.

In ordinary knitting the made sts consist of the following:

yfwd   between two knit stitches
yon   between a purl and knit action
yrn   between two purl actions

In this book the above actions are referred to as m1—make one, as they are commonly written in old lace patterns.

Some helpful abbreviations

k	knit
p	purl
st	stitch
sts	stitches
b	back
f	front
sl	slip
wyib	with yarn in back
wyif	with yarn in front
tog	together
*m1	make one stitch by winding yarn round needle
turn	work is turned before end of row
dpn	double pointed needle
motif	design unit
st st	stocking stitch—knit right side, purl wrong side
garter st	knit all rows
mb	make bobble
beg	beginning
psso	pass slipped stitch over
p2sso	pass 2 slipped stitches over
p-wise	purlwise
k-wise	knitwise

*In old knitting publications the increase in lace knitting was referred to in several different ways: o—over; m1—make one; and cast up.

tbl	through back of loop
ybk	yarn back
yfwd	yarn forward
yon	yarn over needle
yrn	yarn around needle
R.H.	right hand
L.H.	left hand
tw st	twist stitch
inc	increase
dc	double crochet
ch	chain

Comparative terms

British	American
cast off	bind off
tension	gauge
alternate rows	every other row
miss	skip
work straight	work even
stocking stitch	stockinette stitch
shape cap	shape top

Knitting needle sizes

Metric	British	American
2 mm	14	00
2.25	13	0
2.75	12	1
3	11	2
3.25	10	3
3.75	9	4
4	8	5
4.5	7	6
5	6	7
5.5	5	8
6	4	9
6.5	3	10
7	2	10½
7.5	1	11
8	0	12
9	00	13
10	000	15

Victorian grandmother holding an antique Kaiser baby with his shawl of Victoria Point lace (page 84).

Techniques

Casting on

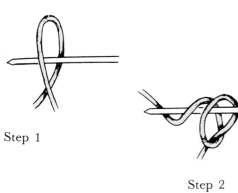

Step 1

Step 2

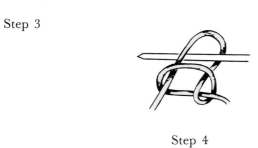

Step 3

Step 4

Thumb method of casting on

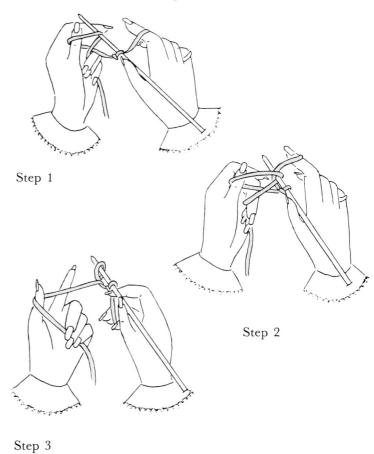

Step 1

Step 2

Step 3

How to knit

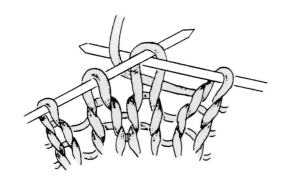

How to purl

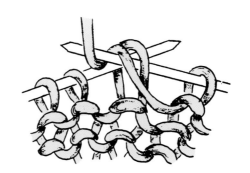

Invisible cast on method

1. Using contrasting thread, cast on the number of stitches required, work two rows in stocking stitch.
2. With main thread, continue work until length required.
3. When work is completed, remove contrasting thread. Either graft or sew together open stitches from both ends of work.

Fig. 2

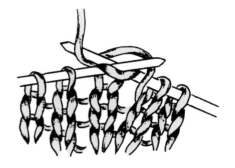

Fig. 3

(a) Make one between two knit stitches

Increasing in lace knitting

There are three methods of increasing the number of stitches on a row, or in a round. One way is to knit twice into a stitch (Fig. 1). This increase can be worked k-wise or p-wise. Read your pattern carefully and work as directed.

A second method is to pick up a loop between two sts, and knit into that loop (Fig. 2). This prevents a hole forming in the knitting.

The third method (Fig. 3), make one (or m1), produces the holes in lace knitting. The way it is worked depends on whether the extra stitch is to be made between two knit stitches, a knit and a purl, or two purl stitches. Between knit sts the yarn is brought forward, and over the needle as you knit the next stitch, thus forming a new stitch. Once again, read your pattern carefully.

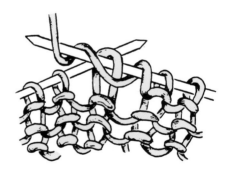

(b) Make one between two purl stitches

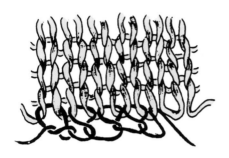

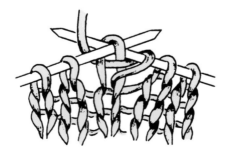

Fig. 1

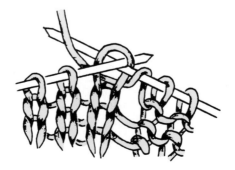

(c) Make one between a knit and a purl stitch

Decreasing in lace knitting

Again there are several methods. One method is to knit or purl two stitches together (Fig. 4a and b). A second method is to pass the second last stitch previously worked over the last one (Fig. 4c and d).

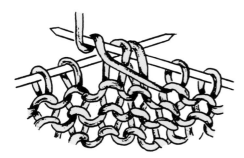

Fig. 4 (a)

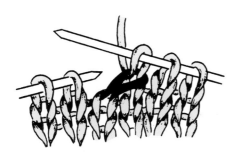

(b)

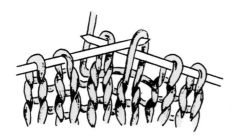

(c)

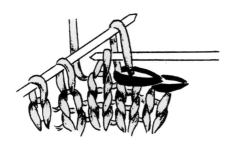

(d)

Knitted picot cast off

Knit 1st st. *Sl 1 st from R.H. needle on to L.H. needle. Insert needle into this st, cast on 2 sts, then cast off 5 sts. Repeat from * until all sts have been cast off.

Knitting off your stitches if you can't crochet

K1, *k2 tog, m1, k2 tog, turn. P1, [(k1, p1) twice, k1] in next stitch.
P1, sl 1 purlwise, turn. Cast off 7 sts (1 st left on R.H. needle)*.
Repeat from *–* to last 5 sts. K3 tog, m1, k2 tog, turn, p1, (k1, p1) twice, k1, in next st, p1, sl 1 purlwise, turn. Cast off remaining sts.
For a larger loop on your edging, make 9 sts instead of the 5 sts described above.

SOME OF THE YARNS USED

(Chart supplied by Amies Tricote)

Brand	Name of yarn	Ply
Anny Blatt	Bombay	10
	Calcutta	7
	Coton d'Egypt	8
	Sao Paulo	8
Missoni	Lipari	3
	Panarea	6
Pinqouin	Cottage	8
	Bambou	6
Schoeller Esslinger	Cobra	8
Schoeller Wolle	Toscana	Size 20
Jaegar	Cotton D.K.	8

Lara (page 22) presiding over the afternoon tea table.

THE PATTERNS

1: MERRIS

Reproduction E.J. doll. 23'' (58.50 cm) by Pat Blyth.
Doll is wearing a two-piece outfit consisting of skirt and braid-trimmed mantle. Approximately
8 × 50 g balls of Anny Blatt Sao Paulo. Pair of 4 mm (8) needles. Blouse and separate
collar worked in DMC Ecru 20 Cotton and 2 mm (14) needles. Ribbon to thread holes and 6
small buttons.

MANTLE

Cast on 36 sts.
Knit (1st row wrong side) until work measures 4½''
(11.25 cm) or sleeve length desired.
Work last row on wrong side.

Shape sides:
Cast on 24 sts at beginning of next 2 rows (84 sts).
Knit 12 rows.

Divide for back and fronts:
Next Row: K42, turn.
K18 rows.
Cast off.
On another needle cast on 42 sts.
For left front K 18 rows (1st row wrong side).
Break off yarn.
Join yarn to remaining 42 sts for back.
K 37 rows.
Next Row: K across all sts (84 sts).
K 12 rows.

Shape sides:
Cast off 24 sts at beginning of next 2 rows (36 sts).
Knit until sleeve measures 4½'' (11.25 cm) working last
row on right side.
Cast off.

This is a one-piece mantle. To edge the garment trim
all edges with lace chain (see page 65 for pattern). The
mantle sits on the doll's shoulders, hanging gracefully.

SKIRT

Cast on 66 sts for back.
Row 1: Knit.
Row 2: Purl.
Row 3: Knit.
Row 4: Purl.
Row 5: Knit.
Repeat rows 1–5 until skirt measures 10'' (25.5 cm) or
length desired.
Continue in st st for 1½'' (4 cm).
Shape paper bag top:
Row 1: Knit.
Row 2: Purl.
Row 3: Sl 1, k1, (m1, k2 tog) to end of row.
Row 4: Purl.
Row 5: Knit.
Row 6: Purl.
Row 7: Sl 1, k1, (m1, k2 tog) to end of row.
Row 8: Purl.

Row 9: Knit.
Row 10: Purl.
Cast off.

Work front as for back.
Press the two sides of the skirt under a damp cloth. Sew
up side seams. Knit 2 lengths of lace chain (see page 65).
St down the side seams. Thread ribbons or cords through
the 2 rows of holes. Draw up evenly. Tie ends in bow.

BLOUSE

Using 2 mm (14) needles, cast on 80 sts.
Work 12 rows k1, p1, rib.
Row 13: Knit inc 1 st (81 sts).
Row 14: Purl.

Proceed in pattern thus, using 2.25 mm (13) needles:
Row 1: K3, (p3, k6) to last 6 sts, p3, k3.
Row 2: P3, (k1, m1, k2 tog, p6) to last 6 sts, k1, m1,
k2 tog, p3.
Row 3: As row 1.
Row 4: Purl.
Row 5: K7, (p3, k6) to last 11 sts, p3, k8.
Row 6: P8, (k1, m1, k2 tog, p6) to last 10 sts, k1, m1,
k2 tog, p7.
Row 7: As row 5.
Row 8: Purl.
Repeat the last 8 rows twice.

Continue thus:
Row 1: Cast off 3 sts, k9, (p3, k6) to last 15 sts, p3, k12.
Row 2: Cast off 3 sts, p9, (k1, m1, k2 tog, p6) to last
12 sts, k1, m1, k2 tog, p9.
Row 3: K2 tog, k7, (p3, k6) to last 12 sts, p3, k7, k2 tog.
Row 4: Purl.
Row 5: K2 tog, k1, (p3, k6) to last 7 sts, p3, k2, k2 tog.
Row 6: P3, (k1, m1, k2 tog, p6) to last 5 sts, k1, m1,
k2 tog, p2.
Row 7: K2 tog, (p3, k6) to last 6 sts, p3, k1, k2 tog.
Row 8: Purl (69 sts).
Row 9: K6, (p3, k6) to end of row.
Row 10: P6, (k1, m1, k2 tog, p6) to end of row.
Row 11: As Row 9.
Row 12: Purl.
Row 13: K1, (p3, k6) to last 5 sts, p3, k2.
Row 14: P2, (k1, m1, k2 tog, p6) to last 4 sts, k1, m1,
k2 tog, p1.
Row 15: As Row 13.
Row 16: Purl.
Repeat the last 8 rows 3 times.
Cast off.

Right front

Using 2 mm (14) needles, cast on 46 sts.
Repeat 1st 12 rows for the back, making a buttonhole in the 7th row thus:
K1, p1, m1, k2 tog, rib to end of row.
Row 13: Knit.
Row 14: P to last 6 sts, k6.

Proceed in pattern thus, using 2.25 mm (13) needles:
Row 1: K13, (p3, k6) to last 6 sts, p3, k3.
Row 2: P3, (k1, m1, k2 tog, p6) to last 16 sts, k1, m1, k2 tog, p7, k6.
Row 3: As Row 1.
Row 4: P to last 6 sts, k6.
Row 5: K8, (p3, k6) to last 11 sts, p3, k8.
Row 6: P8, (k1, m1, k2 tog, p6) to last 11 sts, k1, m1, k2 tog, p2, k6.
Row 7: As Row 5.
Row 8: As Row 4.
Repeat the last 8 rows once making a buttonhole in the 7th row.
Repeat the 8 rows without a buttonhole.

Row 1: Work in pattern to last 15 sts, p3, k12.
Row 2: Cast off 3 sts, p9, (k1, m1, k2 tog, p6) to end of row.
Continue in pattern, dec 1 st at armhole end in next and alternate rows until 40 sts remain.
Work in pattern for 21 rows.

Row 1: Cast off 6 sts, work in pattern to end of row.
Row 2: Work in pattern, dec 1 st at end of row.
Row 3: Cast off 2 sts, work in pattern to end of row.
Repeat the last 2 rows twice.
Continue in pattern, dec 1 st at neck edge of every row until 20 sts remain.
Cast off.

Left front

Using 2 mm (14) needles, cast on 46 sts.
Work as for right front omitting buttonhole on the 7th row.
Row 13: Knit.
Row 14: K6, purl to end of row.

Proceed in pattern thus, using 2.25 mm (13) needles:
Row 1: K3, (p3, k6) to last 16 sts, p3, k13.
Row 2: K6, p7, (k1, m1, k2 tog, p6) to last 6 sts, k1, m1, k2 tog, p3.
Row 3: As Row 1.
Row 4: K6, p to end of row.
Row 5: K8, (p3, k6) to last 11 sts, p3, k8.

Row 6: K6, p2, (k1, m1, k2 tog, p6) to last 11 sts, k1, m1, k2 tog, p8.
Row 7: As Row 5.
Row 8: As Row 4.
Repeat this last 8 rows twice.
Continue in pattern, casting off 3 sts at beginning of next row at armhole edge.
Continue to correspond with right front omitting buttonholes.

Sleeves

Using 2 mm (14) needles, cast on 48 sts.
Work 12 rows k1, p1, rib.
Row 13: K10, (k twice in next st, k1) to last 10 sts, k twice in next st, k9, (63 sts).
Row 14: Purl.
Change to 2.25 mm (13) needles, work in pattern for the back until work measures 6'' (15 cm).
Keeping continuity of pattern, cast off 3 sts at the beginning of the next 2 rows, then dec 1 st at each end of every row until 43 sts remain.
Cast off.

To make up

Press lightly. Sew up seams. Insert sleeves.
Using 2 mm (14) needles pick up and knit 76 sts around the neck.
Row 1: (K1, p1) to end of row.
Row 2: K1, p1, (m1, k2 tog) to the last 2 sts, k2.
Repeat Row 1 twice, cast off.
Thread ribbon through holes, sew on buttons.

ECRU COLLAR

Cast on 101 sts.
Row 1: Knit.
Row 2: Purl.
Row 3: As Row 1.
Row 4: As Row 2.
Row 5: K3, m1, k1, (m1, k2 tog, m1, k1) 14 times, (m1, k2 tog) 3 times, (m1, k1, m1, k2 tog) 16 times, k1 (132 sts).
Row 6: P twice into 1st st, purl to end of row.
Row 7: Knit.
Row 8: Purl.
Row 9: As Row 7.
Row 10: As Row 8.
Row 11: K2, * m1, k2 tog, k1, k2 tog, m1, k1, *. Repeat from * – * to last 11 sts, m1, k2 tog, k1, k2 tog, m1, (k3 tog) twice (129 sts).

Row 12: P3, * m1, p3 tog, m1, p3 *. Repeat from *-* to end of row.
Row 13: K2, k2 tog, * m1, k1, m1, k2 tog, k1, k2 tog *. Repeat from *-* to last 5 sts, m1, k1, m1, k2 tog, k2.
Row 14: P3, * m1, p3, m1, p3 tog *. Repeat from *-* to last 6 sts, (m1, p3) twice (131 sts).
Row 15: K3, * m1, k2 tog, k1, k2 tog, m1, k1, *. Repeat from *-* to last 2 sts, k2.
Row 16: P4, * m1, p3 tog, m1, p3 *. Repeat from *-* to last st, p1.
Row 17: K3, k2 tog, * m1, k1, m1, k2 tog, k1, k2 tog *. Repeat from *-* to last 6 sts, m1, k1, m1, k2 tog, k3.
Row 18: P4, * m1, p3, m1, p3 tog *. Repeat from *-* to last 7 sts, m1, p3, m1, p4 (133 sts).
Row 19: Knit.
Row 20: Purl.
Row 21: As Row 19.
Row 22: As Row 20.
Row 23: K5, k2 tog, * m1, k1, m1, sl 1, k1, psso, k4, k2 tog *. Repeat from *-* to last 9 sts, m1, k1, m1, sl 1, k1, psso, k6.
Row 24: Purl.
Row 25: * Sl 1, k1, psso, k2, k2 tog, m1, k3, m1, *. Repeat from *-* to last 7 sts, sl 1, k1, psso, k2, k3 tog (130 sts).
Row 26: Purl.

Row 27: * Sl 1, k1, psso, k2 tog, m1, k1, m1, k3 tog, m1, k1, m1 *. Repeat from *-* to last 4 sts, sl 1, k1, psso, k2 tog (128 sts).
Row 28: Purl.
Row 29: * K2 tog, m1, k3, m1, k1, m1, k3, m1 *. Repeat from *-* to last 2 sts, k2 tog.
Row 30: Purl.
Row 31: K2, * m1, k3 tog, m1, k3 *. Repeat from *-* to last 5 sts, m1, k3 tog, m1, k2.
Row 32: Purl.

Collar edging

Work 1 dc into 1st 2 sts. Sl 1 off needle, * 6 ch, 1 dc into next 3 sts. Slip off *.
Repeat from *-* to last 2 sts, 6 ch, 1 dc into next 2 sts. Work along row with eight 6 ch loops evenly spaced. Fasten off.
With right side facing, attach thread to 1st row and on other short side of collar 1 dc into same place as join. Continue to work over row ends with eight 6 ch loops evenly spaced, ending with 1 sl st into 1st dc. Fasten off. Work single crochet around neck edge. Press collar. Thread ribbon through 5th row of work. Tie in bow.

The white blouse is from the pattern Lara (next page); the écru blouse and collar on the right are from the pattern Merris on these pages.

2: LARA

Reproduction doll by Lara Blyth 21'' (52 cm).
Full length bannister stitch skirt with a shaped jacket. Approximately 6 × 50 g balls Missoni
Lipari. Jacket knitted on 2.75 mm (12) needles, skirt on 3.25 mm (10) needles. Blouse in
DMC Blanc Size 20 Cotton on 2 mm (14) needles for ribbing and 2.25 mm (13) needles for
the rest. Approximately 2 × 20 g balls. Ribbon to thread through holes at waist and neck.
Six small buttons.

JACKET

Using 2.75 mm (12) needles, cast on 50 sts.

Left front

Row 1: Knit.
Row 2: Purl, inc 1 at each end of needle.
Row 3: Purl.
Row 4: As Row 2.
Row 5: Knit.
Row 6: Knit, inc 1 at each end of needle.
Row 7: Knit.
Row 8: As Row 2.
Row 9: Purl.
Row 10: As Row 2.
Row 11: Knit.
Row 12: Knit, inc 1 at beginning of row.
Row 13: Knit.
Row 14: Purl, inc 1 at beginning of row (62 sts).
Row 15: Purl.

Shape shoulder:
Dec at beginning of next row and of every alternate row, still working in pattern, until there are 53 sts on needle.

Shape armhole:
Cast off 20 sts at shoulder end. Work 8 rows in pattern on the 33 sts that are left. Cast on 20 sts to correspond with the 20 sts that were cast off. Working in pattern, inc at the shoulder every alternate row (62 sts).

Back

Work 27 rows in pattern, then dec at shoulder end in every alternate row (53 sts). Cast off 20 sts for the armhole. Work 8 rows of pattern on the 33 sts that are left. Cast on 20 sts to reach the shoulder.

Right front

Inc in alternate rows at the shoulder end (62 sts).
Dec at shoulder end in next and next alternate row, then dec at both ends of each alternate row (50 sts).
Knit 1 row. Cast off.

Sleeves

Cast on 50 sts. Work in jacket pattern. Dec 1 st at both ends of every 4th row (40 sts).

Work in pattern on these 40 sts until you have worked 52 rows from beginning of sleeve.
Cast off loosely.
Sew up shoulders and sleeve seams. Sew in sleeves.

Frill

Cast on 7 sts on 2.75 mm (12) needles.
Row 1: Knit.
Row 2: K2, p5.
Row 3: K5, turn, p5.
Row 4: K6, turn, k1, p5.
Row 5: P5, k2.
Row 6: Knit.
Row 7: P5, turn, k5.
Row 8: P5, k1, turn, k6.

Repeat rows 1–8 until length required to trim jacket. Make a length of classic cord (see page 63 for pattern). Sew cord on seam, and sleeves. Make a link fastening for jacket waist if desired.

SKIRT

Cast on 150 sts.
Row 1: (K5, p1) to end of row.
Row 2: (K2, p4) to end of row.
Row 3: (K3, p3) to end of row.
Row 4: (K4, p2) to end of row.
Row 5: (K1, p5) to end of row.
Row 6: Knit.
Repeat rows 1–6 until the skirt measures 9½'' (24 cm) or length required.
Next row: (Sl 1, k1, psso, k4) to end of row (125 sts).
Next Row: Knit.
Next Row: (Sl 1, k1, psso, k3) to end of row (100 sts).
Knit 3 rows.
Next Row: (K1, k2 tog). Repeat 11 times, k28, (k2 tog, k1). Repeat 11 times (76 sts).
Knit 3 rows.
Next Row: K1, k2 tog, m1 (buttonhole), k to end of row.
Knit 2 rows.
Cast off.
Sew skirt seam. Sew on button.

BLOUSE

Back

Using 2 mm (14) needles, cast on 78 sts.
Row 1: (K1, p1) to end of row.
Repeat this row 11 times.

Next Row: K14, (k twice in next st, k15) to end of row (82 sts).
Row 14: Purl.

Change to 2.25 mm (13) needles and proceed in pattern as follows:
Row 1: K1, p1, (m1, sl 1, k2 tog, psso, m1, p2) to last 5 sts, m1, sl 1, k2 tog, psso, m1, p1, k1.
Row 2: K2, (p3, k2) to end of row.
Row 3: K1, p1, (k3, p2) to last 5 sts, k3, p1, k1.
Row 4: As Row 2.
Repeat the last 4 rows 6 times.
Keeping continuity of pattern, dec 1 st at each end of next 3 rows, then in alternate rows 3 times.
Work 1 row.
Work 7 patterns. Cast off.

Right front

Cast on 42 sts on 2 mm (14) needles.
Repeat rows 1–12 of back, making a buttonhole in the 7th row thus: k1, p1, m1, k2 tog, rib to end of row.
Row 13: K6, (k twice in next st, k9) to last 6 sts, knit twice in next st, k5 (46 sts).
Row 14: P to last 4 sts, k4.
Proceed in pattern thus:
Row 1: K4, (p2, m1, sl 1, k2 tog, psso, m1) to last 2 sts, p1. k1.
Row 2: (K2, p3) to last 6 sts, k6.
Row 3: K4, (p2, k3) to last 2 sts, p1, k1.
Row 4: As Row 2.
Repeat the last 4 rows 6 times. Make a buttonhole in the 3rd row of the 4th pattern.

Row 1: Work in pattern to last 7 sts, p2, m1, sl 1, k2 tog, psso, k2 tog.
Row 2: P2 tog, p1, work in pattern to end of row.
Row 3: Work in pattern to last 4 sts, p2, k2 tog.
Row 4: K3, p3, (k2, p3) to last 6 sts, k6.
Row 5: K4, (p2, m1, sl 1, k2 tog, psso, m1) to last 3 sts, p1, k2 tog.
Row 6: (K2, p3) to last 6 sts, k6.
Row 7: K4, (p2, k3) to last 2 sts, k2 tog.
Row 8: K1, p3, (k2, p3) to last 6 sts, k6.
Row 9: K4, p2, (m1, sl 1, k2 tog, psso, m1, p2) to last 4 sts, m1, sl 1, k1, psso, k2 tog.
Row 10: K1, p2, (k2, p3) to last 6 sts, k6.
Row 11: K4, (p2, k3) to end of row.
Row 12: As Row 10.
Row 13: K2, m1, k2 tog, (p2, m1, sl 1, k2 tog, psso, m1) to last 5 sts, p2, m1, sl 1, k1, psso, k1.
Row 14: As Row 10.
Row 15: As Row 11.
Row 16: As Row 10.

Row 17: K4, (p2, m1, sl 1, k2 tog, psso, m1) to last 5 sts, m1, sl 1, k1, psso, k1.
Row 18: As Row 10.

Repeat the last 4 rows twice.
Proceed as follows:
Row 1: Cast off 6 sts, work in pattern to end of row.
Row 2: Work in pattern to last 2 sts, k2 tog.
Row 3: Cast off 2 sts, work in pattern to end of row.
Repeat the last 2 rows twice.
Continue in pattern and dec 1 st at neck edge in next 4 rows (20 sts).
Work 1 row. Cast off.

Left front

Cast on 42 sts and work as right front for first 12 rows, omitting the buttonhole.
Row 13: K5, (k twice in next st, k9) to last 6 sts, k6.
Row 14: K4, purl to end of row.
Proceed as follows:
Row 1: (P2, m1, sl 1, k2 tog, psso, m1) to last 6 sts, p2, k4.
Row 2: K6, (p3, k2) to end of row.
Row 3: (P2, k3) to last 6 sts, p2, k4.
Row 4: As Row 2.
Continue to correspond with right side, omitting buttonholes, and reversing armhole and neck shapings.

Sleeves

Using 2 mm (14) needles, cast on 48 sts.
Work 10 rows k1, p1, rib.
Row 11: K11, (k twice in next st, k2) to last 13 sts, k twice in next st, k12 (57 sts).
Row 12: Purl.
Change to 2.25 mm (13) needles, work in back pattern until sleeve measures 6'' (15 cm) or length required.
Keeping continuity of pattern, cast off 3 sts at beginning of next 2 rows, then dec 1 st at each end of every row until 37 sts remain.
Cast off.

To make up blouse

Press lightly, sew up seams, insert sleeves.
With right side of work facing and using 2 mm (14) needles, pick up and knit 76 sts along neck edge.
Row 1: (K1, p1) to end of row.
Row 2: K1, p1, m1, k2 tog, rib to end of row.
Repeat Row 1 twice, cast off.
Thread ribbon through holes, sew on buttons.

3: VIOLA

Antique doll by Hamburger, Berlin, circa 1903, 26'' (66 cm).
Lace-trimmed shrug and fluted skirt in Anny Blatt Calcutta yarn. 2.75 mm (12) and
3.25 mm (10) needles for shrug. Skirt, 3.25 mm (10) needles. Lace around shrug, 4 mm (8)
needles. Approximately 10 × 50 g balls of Calcutta (7 ply). Length of elastic for waist.
Ribbon to tie at wrists.
Doll from author's collection.

SHRUG

Cast on 33 sts using 2.75 mm (12) needles.
Knit 3 rows.
Next Row: K2, (m1, k2 tog) to end of row.
Knit 3 rows.
Next Row: K4, * inc in next st. repeat from * to last 5 sts, k5 (57 sts).
Change to 3.25 mm (10) needles and work in garter stitch for 16'' (41 cm).
Next Row: K4, * k2 tog. Repeat from * to last 5 sts, k5.
Change to 2.75 mm (12) needles and knit 3 rows.
Next Row: K2, (m1, k2 tog) to end of row.
Knit 3 rows.
Cast Off.

Shrug lace

Using 4 mm (8) needles, cast on 8 sts.
Row 1: Sl 1, k1, (m1, k2 tog) twice, m1, k2.
Row 2 and alternate rows: Sl 1, k to end of row.
Row 3: Sl 1, k2, (m1, k2 tog) twice, m1, k2.
Row 5: Sl 1, k3, (m1, k2 tog) twice, m1, k2.
Row 7: Sl 1, k4, (m1, k2 tog) twice, m1. k2.
Row 8: Sl 1, k to end of row.
Row 9: Sl 1, k11.
Row 10: Cast off 4 sts, k to end of row (8 sts).
Repeat rows 1–10 until lace is long enough to go around shrug, allowing ample fullness where necessary.
Press shrug lightly. Thread ribbon through holes. Tie around arms of doll on inside of shrug. Fold back lace around top of shrug to form collar.

SKIRT

Cast on 72 sts.
Row 1: Knit.
Row 2: Sl 1, k65, (m1, k2 tog) twice, m1, k2.
Row 3: Sl 1, k8, p48, turn leaving 16 sts on needle.
Row 4: Sl 1, k50, (m1, k2 tog) twice, m1, k2.
Row 5: Sl 1, k9, p48, k16.
Row 6: Sl 1, k67, (m1, k2 tog) twice, m1, k2.
Row 7: Sl 1, k10, p48, turn leaving 16 sts on needle.
Row 8: Sl 1, p47, k5, (m1, k2 tog) twice, m1, k2.
Row 9: Sl 1, k75.
Row 10: Sl 1, k15, p48, k6, (m1, k2 tog) twice, m1, k2.
Row 11: Sl 1, k60, turn leaving 16 sts on needle.
Row 12: Sl 1, p47, k7, (m1, k2 tog) twice, m1, k2.
Row 13: Cast off 6 sts. K to end of row.

Repeat rows 2–13 30 times, or more if required.
Cast off. Join back seam. Use a length of wide elastic to thread through casing. Fold over band and sl st into position.
Length of skirt can be adjusted by increasing or reducing the number of sts in the ribbed section.

4: CARA WILKIE-DAVEY

Reproduction 'Fleur' doll by Pat Blyth 22'' (56 cm).
Doll is wearing an eyelet skirt with a cross-over top. A full-length boa completes the ensemble.
Knitted in Missoni Lipari, approximately 8 × 50 g balls. Jacket on 2.75 mm (12) needles.
Skirt on 3.25 mm (10) needles. Boa on 3 mm (11) needles.

JACKET

Cast on 52 sts. Knit 6 rows.
Proceed as follows:
Row 1: Knit.
Row 2: K1, purl to last st. k1.
Repeat rows 1 and 2 until work measures 6'' (15 cm) or length required for your doll. End with purl row.
Inc at each end of needle in next, and every alternate row until there are 60 sts on needle.
Cast on 14 sts at end of each of next 2 rows.
Work 2'' (5 cm) in st st making an edge of 4 garter sts at each end of work.
End with a knit row.

Continue as follows:
Row 1: K4, p28, k24, p28, k4.
Row 2: Knit.
Repeat these two rows twice.
Row 7: K4, p28, k4, cast off 16, k4, p28, k4.
Continue on the last 36 sts as follows:
Row 1: Knit.
Row 2: K4, p28, k4.
Repeat these two rows twice.
Continue in st st, keeping an edge of 4 garter sts at each end of needle and increasing once at the neck edge in every row (inside garter st border) until there are 54 sts on needle.
Cast off 14 sts at beginning of next row.
Continue increasing at neck edge in every row, at the same time decreasing at armhole edge in every knit row until 4 decreasings have been worked.
Continue to inc in every row at front edge until there are 50 sts on needle.
Work without shaping until front measures same as back.
Cast off.
Work on other 36 sts to correspond.
Cast off.

Make up

Press work lightly. Sew up side and underarm seams. Lap right front over left. Sew on ribbons, make a bow just above garter stitch and 2'' (5 cm) above; a third bow can be added if desired. A fine ribbon tie at the inside right seam holds jacket in place.

SKIRT

Cast on 164 sts.
Row 1: (K1, p1) to end of row.
Row 2 (right side of work): Purl.
Row 3: Purl.
Row 4: (M1, sl 1, k1, psso) to end of row.
Row 5: Purl.
Repeat rows 2–5 until skirt measures 9½'' (24 cm), ending with Row 5 (adjust length of skirt if required).
Next Row: (P2 tog) to end of row (82 sts).
Continue in k1, p1, rib for approximately 1½'' (4 cm).
Make a row of holes thus:
K2, (m1, k2 tog) to end of row.
Continue in k1, p1, rib for 6 rows.
Cast off.
Sew skirt together. Thread elastic through holes. Adjust to doll's waist. Tape or ribbon could be used if desired.

BOA

Cast on 10 sts. Knit 1 row.
Row 1: Sl 1, insert righthand needle in next st as if you were going to knit it. Pass yarn over point and around 1st and 2nd fingers of left hand 3 times, and over point of needle. Knit all 4 threads of cotton in as you knit the st, knit 7 sts in same manner, k1.
Row 2: Sl 1, knit working every group of threads as 1 st, drawing the thread through tightly.
Repeat these 2 rows until length desired.

5: PEGGY

Reproduction doll by Pat Blyth 24'' (61 cm).
Doll is wearing a long skirt and top in Missoni Lipari. Approximately 6 × 50 g balls. Top worked on 2.75 mm (12) needles. Skirt on 3.25 mm needles. Length of elastic for skirt waist. 5 buttons for top. Peggy wears a cravat fashioned from a length of antique ribbon.

JACKET

Back

Using 2.75 mm (12) needles, cast on 67 sts.
Row 1: K2, * p1, k1, repeat from * to last st, k1.
Row 2: K1, * p1, k1, repeat from * to end of row.
Repeat Rows 1 and 2 eight times.
Change to 3.25 mm (10) needles and work in st st until work measures 5'' or length required, ending with a purl row.

Shape armholes:
Cast off 4 sts at beginning of next 2 rows, then dec at each end of next and alt rows until 53 sts remain.
Work 27 st st rows.

Shape shoulders:
Cast off 8 sts at beginning of next 2 rows, then 7 sts at beginning of following 2 rows.
Cast off remaining 23 sts.

Front

Work as for back, dec 1 st in centre of last row of ribbing (66 sts).
Change to 3.25 mm (10) needles, and work in st st until there are 12 rows less than back to underarm, ending with purl row.

Divide for front:
Row 1: K33, turn.
Row 2: K2, p to end of row.
Work 10 rows on these 33 sts, working 2 sts in garter st at front edge.

Shape armhole:
Cast off 4 sts at beginning of next row.
Decrease at armhole edge in alternate rows until 26 sts remain.
Work 10 rows.

Shape neck:
Row 1: Cast off 6 sts, p to end of row.
Dec at neck edge in next and alternate rows until 15 sts remain.
Work 7 rows.

Shape top:
Cast off 8 sts at beginning of next row.
Work 1 row.
Cast off.

Join yarn to remaining sts, work the other side to correspond.

Sleeves

Using 2.75 mm (12) needles, cast on 122 sts for frilled edge of cuff.
Continue as follows:
***Row 1:* * P2, k6, repeat from * to last 2 sts, p2.
Row 2: K2, * p6, k2, repeat from * to end of row.
Row 3: * P2, sl 1, k1, psso, k2, k2 tog, repeat from * to last 2 sts, p2 (92 sts).
Row 4: K2, * p4, k2, repeat from * to end of row.
Row 5: * P2, sl 1, k1, psso, k2 tog, repeat from * to last 2 sts, p2 (62 sts).
Row 6: K2, * p2, k2, repeat from * to end of row.
Row 7: * P2, k2 tog, repeat from * to last 2 sts, p2, **.
Row 8: Purl (47 sts).
Work 27 rows of ribbing as for the back.

Change to 3.25 mm (10) needles, work 4 rows st st beginning with a knit row, to reverse fabric of sleeve.
Row 5: K2, inc 1, k to last 2 sts, inc 1, k2.
Inc as before in following 4th rows until there are 57 sts on needle.
Continue until sleeve measures 7'' (18 cm) from cast on edge of frill, or length desired, ending with a purl row.

Shape top:
Cast off 2 sts at beginning of next 2 rows.
Decrease at each end of next and alternate rows until 41 sts remain, then in every row until 15 sts remain.
Cast off.

Collar

Cast on 298 sts on 2.75 mm (12) needles.
Work as from **-** for sleeves (113 sts).
Row 8: P13, (p1, p2 tog tbl) twice, p74, p2 tog, p1, (p2 tog) twice, turn.
Row 9: K80, sl 1, k1, psso, turn.
Row 10: P80, p2 tog, turn.
Row 11: K1, k2 tog, k75, (sl 1, k1, psso) twice, turn.
Row 12: P78, p2 tog, turn.
Row 13: K78, sl 1, k1, psso, turn.
Repeat rows 12 and 13 five times, then row 12 once (90 sts).
Row 25: K2, k2 tog, k2, * k2 tog, k4, repeat from * to last 13 sts, k2 tog, k2, k2 tog, sl 1, k1, psso, turn (75 sts).
Row 26: P64, p2 tog, turn.
Row 27: K64, sl 1, k1, psso, turn.
Row 28: P8, (k1, p1) 24 times, k1, p7, p2 tog, turn.

Row 29: K8, (p1, k1) 24 times, p1, k7, sl 1, k1, psso, turn.
Repeat rows 28 and 29 twice, then row 28 once.
Cast off.

Jabot

Cast on 146 sts on 2.75 mm (12) needles.
Work as from **–** for sleeves (56 sts).
Row 8: P28, p2 tog, turn.
Row 9: K1, sl 1, k1, psso, turn.
Row 10: P2, p2 tog, turn.
Row 11: K3, sl 1, k1, psso, turn.
Row 12: P4, p2 tog, turn.
Row 13: K5, sl 1, k1, psso, turn.
Row 14: P5, p2 tog, turn.
Repeat rows 13 and 14 until 7 sts remain.
Cast off.

Make up

Press work lightly avoiding frills and ribbing. Join
shoulder, side and sleeve seams, taking care to reverse
seam on sleeve frill and ¾ of ribbing for turn back of
cuff. Sew sleeves into armholes, sew collar in position,
adjusting seam evenly. Place front band of jabot to cover
opening, and sew down right side, across the bottom,
and for approx ½'' (1 cm) up the left side. Use press
studs to close. Make a loop, and attach button to top of
band. Sew a row of buttons to decorate front panel of
jabot. Lightly press finished garment.

SKIRT

Back

Cast on 134 sts.
Row 1 (right side): (K2, p2) to last 2 sts, k2.
Row 2: P2, (k2, p2) to end of row.
Continue working in k2, p2, rib until work measures 9''
(23 cm) or length required.
End with row 1.
Decrease thus:
P2, (k2 tog, p2 tog) to last 4 sts, k2 tog, p2.

Waistband

Beginning with a k row, work in st st for 2'' (5 cm).
Cast off loosely.

Front

Work as for back.

Make up

Join side seams. Cut elastic to doll's waist measurement.
Overlap ends forming a ring and sew securely. Fold
waistband in half to wrong side enclosing elastic. Sl st
cast-off edge into place.

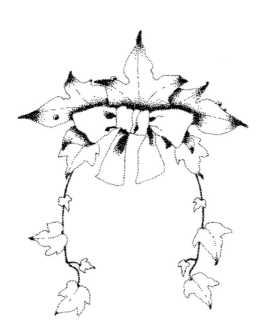

6: BLACK OPAL

Antique Simon & Halbig 22'' (56 cm).
Doll is wearing a black Missoni Lipari two-piece outfit. Jacket and skirt worked on 2.75 mm (12) needles. Approximately 6 × 50 g balls. Suit worn over an antique white blouse. Knitted mittens (see page 67 for pattern).
Doll from author's collection.

JACKET

Back

Cast on 58 sts.
Knit 4 rows.
Row 5: Sl 1, k1, (m1, k2 tog) to end of row.
Row 6: Sl 1, p1, (k2, p2) to end of row.
Row 7: Sl 1, k1, (p2, k2) to end of row.
Row 8: As Row 6.
Repeat Rows 7–8 until 13 rows of rib are completed.
Knit 1 row.
Purl 1 row.
Row 21: Sl 1, k1, (m1, k2 tog) to end of row.
Row 22: Knit.
Row 23: Knit.
Row 24: Purl.
Repeat the last 4 rows 10 times (11 lines of holes).
Row 65: Sl 1, k1, (p2, k2) to end of row.
Row 66: Sl 1, p1, (k2, p2) to end of row.
Repeat rows 65–66 5 times.
Next Row: Knit.
Next Row: Purl.
This completes the back.

Work right shoulder:
Row 1: Sl 1, k1, (m1, k2 tog) 7 times, k1, turn.
Row 2: K17.
Row 3: Knit.
Row 4: Purl.
Repeat the last 4 rows until you have worked 30 rows.
Slip sts on spare needle or holder.

Front

Next Row: K17 shoulder sts. Cast on 17 sts right side of front.
Next Row: K17, p17, k34 on needle.
Row 1: Sl 1, k1, (p2, k2) 6 times, p2, k6.
Row 2: Sl 1, k7, p2, (k2, p2) to end of row.
Repeat these 2 rows until 12 rows of ribbing are done. When you get to the edge sts of the 7th row make a buttonhole thus: K3, Draw the last but 1 over the last st, k1. Draw another st over, k the last 2 sts. In the next row cast on 2 sts to replace those cast off.
Row 13: Knit.
Row 14: K6, p28.
Row 15: Sl 1, k1, (m1, k2 tog) 12 times, k6.
Row 16: Knit.
Row 17: Knit.
Row 18: K6, p28.
Repeat the last 4 rows 10 times (11 lines of holes). Form a buttonhole every 12 rows.

Row 59: Sl 1, k1, (p2, k2) 6 times, p2, k6.
Row 60: Sl 1, k7, p2, (k2, p2) to end of row.
Repeat the last 2 rows until 12 rows of ribbing are done.
Next Row: Sl 1, k1, (m1, k2 tog) 12 times, k6.
Knit 4 rows.
Cast off.

Resume where you divided for the shoulder. Cast off 24 sts across the back of the jacket, k2. You now have 3 sts on R.H. needle, 15 sts on L.H. needle. (M1, k2 tog) 7 times.
Row 2 of shoulder: Knit (17 sts).
Row 3: Knit.
Row 4: Purl.
Continue in open pattern to correspond with 1st shoulder until 30 rows are done. At the end of the 30th row cast on 17 sts (34 sts).
Next Row: Knit.
Next Row: Purl.
Row 1: Beginning at front edge k6, (p2, k2) to end of row.
Row 2: (P2, k2) 6 times, p2, k8.
Repeat these 2 rows until 12 rows of ribbing are done.
Row 13: Knit.
Row 14: P28, k6.
Row 15: K6, (m1, k2 tog) to end of row.
Row 16: Knit.
Row 17: Knit.
Row 18: P28, k6.
Repeat the last 4 rows 10 times (11 lines of holes).
Row 59: K6, (p2, k2) to end of row.
Row 60: (P2, k2) 6 times, p2, k8.
Repeat the last 2 rows until 12 rows of ribbing are done.
Next Row: K6, (m1, k2 tog) to end of row.
Knit 4 rows.
Cast off.

Sleeves

Pick up 40 sts along armhole edge.
Row 1: Knit.
Row 2: Purl.
Row 3: Sl 1, k1, (m1, k2 tog) to end of row.
Row 4: Knit.
Row 5: K2 tog, k to last 2 sts, k2 tog.
Row 6: P2 tog, p to last 2 sts, p2 tog (36 sts).
Row 7: Sl 1, k1, (m1, k2 tog) to end of row.
Row 8: Knit.
Row 9: Knit.
Row 10: Purl.
Repeat the last 4 rows 9 times (11 lines of holes).
Work 16 rows in k2, p2, rib.
Cast off.
Sew sleeve and side seams.
Pick up and knit sts around neck.

Knit 2 rows.
Next Row: Sl 1, k1, (m1, k2 tog) to end of row.
Knit 2 rows.
Use picot cast off.
Sew on buttons. Thread ribbons through holes at neck and waist. Tie ends in bows.

SKIRT

Cast on 152 sts for back.
Row 1: (K7, p1) to end of row.
Row 2: K4, (p1, k7) to last 4 sts, p1, k3.
Repeat rows 1–2 until skirt measures 9½ '' (24 cm).
Next Row: (K2 tog) to end of row.

Waistband

Row 1: Knit.
Row 2: Purl.
Row 3: Sl 1, k1, (m1, k2 tog) to end of row.
Row 4: Purl.
Row 5: Knit.
Row 6: Purl.
Row 7: Sl 1, k1, (m1, k2 tog) to end of row.
Row 8: Purl.
Row 9: Knit.
Row 10: Purl.
Cast off.
Work front as for back.
Sew up side seams. Thread ribbons through holes at the waist. Adjust to doll's waist. Tie in bow.

7: VILMA

Antique Simon & Halbig K * R 22'' (56 cm).
Doll is wearing a full-length black gown. The full skirt is scattered with knitted leaves. The cape is worked in 4 sections until the neckline. Use 3 mm (11) needles and a set of double-pointed 2 mm (14) needles. Approximately 6 × 50 g balls of Missoni Lipari.
Doll from Blyth collection.

CAPE

Cast on 103 sts (k 1st and last st in every row).
Row 1: Purl.
Row 2: Knit.
Row 3: Purl.
Row 4: K1, (m1, k2 tog) to end of row.
Row 5: Purl.
Row 6: Knit.
Row 7: Purl.
Row 8: Knit.
Row 9: Purl.

Shaping

Row 1: K1, sl 1, k2 tog, psso, k46, sl 1, k2 tog, psso, k46, sl 1, k2 tog, psso, k1.
Row 2: K1, sl 1, k2 tog, psso, k43, sl 1, k2 tog, psso, k43, sl 1, k2 tog, psso, k1.
Row 3: Purl.
Row 4: Knit.
Row 5: Purl.
Dec every 4th row, knitting 3 sts less either side of central decrease until cape measures 8'' (20 cm) along central decrease. Leave sts on spare needle (25 sts).
Work 3 more pieces the same.
Place sts evenly on 4 double-pointed needles. Work with 5th needle.
Knit 1½'' (3 cm).
Next Round: K1, (m1, k2 tog) to end of round.
Next Round: Purl.
Next Round: Knit.
Next Round: Purl.
Cast off.

Make up

Press lightly. Sew sections together from top to bottom end. Press each seam. Turn up hem. Neatly sl st into place. Turn under top of cape. Sl st the hem. Knit 3 buttons, place on centre seam.

Knit buttons thus:
Cast on 10 st.
Row 1: K1, (m1, k1) to end of row.
Repeat Row 1 twice. Cast off. Shape into buttons and stitch to garment.
Knitted leaves trim the skirt of the dress.

Long leaf

Cast on 1 st.
Row 1: M1, k1, m1.
Row 2: Purl, and every alternate row.
Row 3: (K1, m1) twice, k1.
Row 5: K2, m1, k1, m1, k2.
Row 7: K3, m1, k1, m1, k3.
Row 9: K1, sl 1, k1, psso, (k1, m1) twice, k4.
Row 11: K1, sl 1, k1, psso, (k1, m1) twice, k5.
Row 13: K1, sl 1, k1, psso, k8.
Row 15: K1, sl 1, k1, psso, k7.
Row 17: K1, sl 1, k1, psso, k6.
Row 19: K1, sl 1, k1, psso, k5.
Row 21: K1, sl 1, k1, psso, k4.
Row 23: K1, sl 1, k1, psso, k3.
Row 25: K1, sl 1, k1, psso, k2
Row 27: K1, sl 1, k1, psso, k1.
Row 29: K1, k2 tog.
Row 31: K2 tog.
Row 32: P1.
Row 33: K1.
Row 34: P1.
Cast off. Repeat rows 1–34 to complete each leaf motif.

Back view of Lily's shoulder cape and train (facing page).

8: LILY

Doll carved by Jan Clements of Yackandandah 20'' (51 cm).
Doll is wearing a hand-tucked antique muslin skirt and top. Her train and shoulder cape are knitted in DMC Blanc 20 cotton. Use 2 mm (14), 2.75 mm (12) and 3.75 mm (10) needles. The bridal bonnet also in DMC 20 Blanc on 2 mm (14) needles. Approximately 8 balls of cotton. Ribbon for the bonnet and cape.
Doll from author's collection.

BRIDAL TRAIN

Cast on 66 sts using 2.75 mm (12) needles.
Row 1: Knit.
Row 2: Purl.
Repeat rows 1–2.
Row 5: Knit.
Repeat rows 1–5 until you have 23 raised and 22 depressed ribs. Cast off. The side that commences and ends with a raised rib is the right side of train.

Insertion

Cast on 161 sts.
Knit 5 rows.
Row 1: K7, * sl 1, k1, psso, m1, k2 tog, k7, repeat from * to end of row.
Row 2: Purl.
Row 3: K6, * sl 1, k1, psso, m1, k1, m1, k2 tog, k5, repeat from * to last st, k1.
Row 4: Purl.
Row 5: K5, * sl 1, k1, psso, m1, k3, m1, k2 tog, k3, repeat from * to last 2 sts, k2.
Row 6: Purl.
Row 7: K4, * sl 1, k1, psso, m1, k5, m1, k2 tog, k1, repeat from * to last 3 sts, k3.
Row 8: Purl.
End of insertion:
Knit 4 rows. Cast off.
Sew insertion to bottom of train.

Lace edging

Cast on 11 sts.
Row 1: Sl 1, k2 tog, m1, k1, (m1, k2 tog) 3 times, m1, k1.
Row 2 and alternate rows: Knit.
Row 3: Sl 1, k2 tog, m1, k2, (m1, k2 tog) 3 times, m1, k1.
Row 5: Sl 1, k2 tog, m1, k3, (m1, k2 tog) 3 times, m1, k1.
Row 7: Sl 1, k2 tog, m1, k4, (m1, k2 tog) 3 times, m1, k1.
Row 9: Sl 1, k2 tog, m1, k5, (m1, k2 tog) 3 times, m1, k1.
Row 11: Sl 1, k2 tog, m1, k6, (m1, k2 tog) 3 times, m1, k1.
Row 12: Cast off 6 sts, k10.
Repeat Rows 1–12 until sufficient length to trim train, making sure lace curves around insertion. Sew neatly to train. Make 8 ribbon bows and sew across seam line. Thread fine cord through waist. Tie in front.

Shoulder cape

Cast on 66 sts using 2 mm (14) needles.
Knit in rib pattern as for train.
Omit insertion.
Work a length of lace as for train. Sew lace to cape.

Knit 2 lengths of lace of approximately 7 patterns each. Gather cape at neck, threading through fine cord. Thread fine ribbon through lengths of lace and gather to form a double frill around neck.
Tie ribbon in a bow.

BRIDAL BONNET

Cast on 22 sts.
K 48 rows.
Cast on 23 sts at each end of next row.
Knit 6 rows.
Make a row of holes:
K2, (m2, k2 tog, k2) to end of row.
Next Row: Knit, dropping 1 loop of m2 of previous row.
Knit 6 rows.
Row of holes as before.
Knit 6 rows.
Row of holes as before.
Knit 12 rows.
Cast on 6 sts at each end of row.
Knit 18 rows. Cast off.
Sew sides to back. The 6 added sts at each end come below the bonnet.
Pick up and knit sts across bottom of bonnet.
Make a row of holes as before.
Knit 12 rows. Cast off.

Bonnet frills

Back frill:
Cast on 86 sts.
Row 1: Knit.
Row 2: (M1, k1) to end of row.
Row 3: Knit.
Row 4: (M1, k1) to end of row.
Row 5 and 6: Knit.
Cast off loosely.

Front frill:
Cast on 146 sts.
Work as for back frill. Cast off.
Sew to front of bonnet, catching the cast on sts, easing any fullness.
Sew back frill around back of bonnet crown. Sew another frill at neck piece of bonnet. The frills will fall into place if correctly attached.

Thread ribbons through the 3 rows of holes in bonnet front. Thread ribbon through holes in neck leaving sufficient length to tie into bow under chin if desired. Turn back bonnet front and frilled edge to frame face. Ribbon rosettes could be used as a trim at sides.

9: ROSAMUNDA

Reproduction bust by Pat Blyth.
Collar hand made by Kathie Savage. Lace knitted by author using DMC 100 Cotton on
1 mm (20) needles. Approximately 1 ball.

Cast on 8 sts.
Row 1: Sl 1, k1, (m1, p2 tog, (k1, p1, k1) in next st) twice.
Row 2: (K3, m1, p2 tog) twice, k2.

Row 3: Sl 1, k1, (m1, p2 tog, k3) twice.
Row 4: (Cast off 2 sts, m1, p2 tog) twice, k2.
Repeat Rows 1–4 until length desired.

10: CAPRICORNIA

Antique Jumeau doll 21'' (53 cm).
Collar made by Kathie Savage. Lace knitted by author using DMC 100 Cotton on 1 mm (20)
needles. Approximately 1 × 20 g ball.
Doll from Blyth collection.

Cast on 8 sts.
Row 1: Sl 1, k2, m1, k2 tog, m2, k2 tog, k1.
Row 2: K3, p1, k2, m1, k2 tog, k1.
Row 3: Sl 1, k2, m1, k2 tog, k1, m2, k2 tog, k1.
Row 4: K3, p1, k3, m1, k2 tog, k1.

Row 5: Sl 1, k2, m1, k2 tog, k2, m2, k2 tog, k1.
Row 6: K3, p1, k4, m1, k2 tog, k1.
Row 7: Sl 1, k2, m1, k2 tog, k6.
Row 8: Cast off 3 sts, k4, m1, k2 tog, k1.
Repeat Rows 1–8 until length desired.

11: CHERRY

Reproduction doll by Aileen Sellen 18'' (46 cm).
Doll is wearing white lace with cherry ribbons. You will need approximately 5 × 20 g DMC
Blanc 5200, 1 mm (20) and 3 mm (11) needles.
Doll from author's collection.

DRESS

Cast on 242 sts using 3 mm (11) needles.
Row 1: Knit.
Row 2: Purl.
Row 3: Knit.
Row 4: K2 tog tbl, * k3, m1, k1, m1, k3, (k2 tog) twice, repeat from * to end of row.
Row 5: Purl.
Row 6: As Row 4.
Row 7: As Row 5.
Row 8: As Row 4.
Row 9: Knit.
Row 10: Purl.
Row 11: Knit.
Repeat Rows 4–11 twice.
Row 28: Knit.
Row 29: Sl 1, * p3 tog, (k1, p1, k1) in next st, repeat from * to last st, k1.
Row 30: Purl.
Row 31: Sl 1, * (k1, p1, k1) in next st, p3 tog, repeat from * to end of row.
Row 32: Purl.
Repeat the last 4 rows 7 times.
Purl next row.

Continue in twist st:
Row 1: K2, k in back of 2nd st and front of 1st st, slip both off the needle, k2. Repeat to end of row.
Row 2: Purl.
Repeat last 2 rows 12 times.

Shape waist

Row 1: K2, k2 tog. Repeat to end of row (122 sts)
Row 2: Knit.
Row 3: As Row 2.
Row 4: * M1, k2 tog, k2, repeat from * to last 4 sts, k4.
Row 5: Purl.
Rows 6–9: Knit.
Continue in twist pattern for 8 rows.

K34, turn, purl back. Continue on these 34 sts for left back. Work 28 rows. Leave sts on spare needle.
Knit 54 for front. Work on these 54 sts until same length as back. Leave sts on spare needle.
Work the last 34 sts for right back to correspond with left back. Place all sts on one needle, knit 4 rows.
Next Row: (K2, m1, k2 tog) to end of row.
Knit 4 rows.
Cast off.

Sleeves

Cast on 36 sts.
Work in k1, p1, rib for 6 rows.
Work in twist pattern 1½'' (4 cm). Inc 1 st at end of every 4th row until you have 40 sts. Work until sleeve measures 4'' (10 cm). Cast off.

Sew sleeve seams and sew into armholes. Crochet around neck, and back opening thus: 2 dc, 2 ch, 2 dc. Thread ribbons through holes at neck and waist. Tie at back.

12: NET LACE

A simple lace knitted as a skirt flounce. The flounce was knitted in DMC 20 Cotton on 1.75 mm (15) needles.

Cast on 31 sts.
Row 1: Sl 1, k1, k2 tog, m2, k2 tog, k1, (m1, k2 tog) twice, k2 tog, m2, k2 tog, k1, m2, k2 tog, (m1, k2 tog) 6 times, k1.
Row 2: K15, p1, k3, p1, k8, p1, k3.

Row 3: Sl 1, k6, (m1, k2 tog) twice, k5, m2, k2 tog, (m1, k2 tog) 6 times, m1, k2.
Row 4: Cast off 3 sts, k13, p1, k16.
Repeat Rows 1-4 until length desired.

13: ROSE WHITE

Rose White lingerie fashioned to eliminate angles and curves, and enhanced with fine knitting using DMC 100 Cotton and 1 mm (20) needles. The five lace edgings on the garments are complemented with tiny feather stitching. Information on Rose White Designs can be found in the list of suppliers.

Doll is an antique A.M. 900 from author's collection.

LARISSA

Cast on 5 sts.
Row 1: Sl 1, k1, k2 tog, m1, k1.
Row 2: K1, (k1, p1, k1, p1, k1) in next st, m1, k2 tog, k1.
Row 3: Sl 1, k1, m1, k2 tog, k5.
Row 4: K6, m1, k2 tog, k1.
Row 5: As Row 3.
Row 6: As Row 4.
Row 7: As Row 3.
Row 8: Cast off 4 sts, k1, m1, k2 tog, k1.
Repeat Rows 1-8 until length desired.

GILLIAN

Cast on 4 sts.
Row 1: Sl 1, k1, m1, k2.
Row 2: K5.
Row 3: Sl 1, k2, m1, k2.
Row 4: K6.
Row 5: Sl 1, k1, m2, k2 tog, m1, k2.
Row 6: K5, p1, k2.
Row 7: Sl 1, k5, m1, k2.
Row 8: Cast off 5 sts, k3.
Repeat Rows 1-8 until length desired.

SANDRA

Cast on 5 sts.
Row 1: M1, p2 tog, k1, m2, k2.
Row 2: K2, (k1, p1, k1) in m2 of previous row, k1, m1, p2 tog.
Row 3: M1, p2 tog, k6.
Row 4: K6, m1, p2 tog.
Row 5: M1, p2 tog, k6.
Row 6: Cast off 3 sts, k2, m1, p2 tog.
Repeat Rows 1-6 until length desired.

ALISON

Cast on 4 sts.
Row 1: Knit.
Row 2: K1, m1, k2 tog, m2, k1.
Row 3: K2, p1, k1, m1, k2 tog.
Row 4: K1, m1, k2 tog, k3.
Row 5: Cast off 2 sts, k1, m1, k2 tog.
Repeat Rows 2-5 until length desired.

JANINE

Cast on 5 sts.
Row 1: Sl 1, k1, m2, k2 tog, k1.
Row 2: Sl 1, k2, p1, k2.
Row 3: Sl 1, k3, m2, k2.
Row 4: Sl 1, k2, p1, k4.
Row 5: Sl 1, k1, m2, k2 tog, k4.
Row 6: Sl 1, k5, p1, k2.
Row 7: Sl 1, k8.
Row 8: Cast off 4 sts, k4.
Repeat Rows 1-8 until length desired.

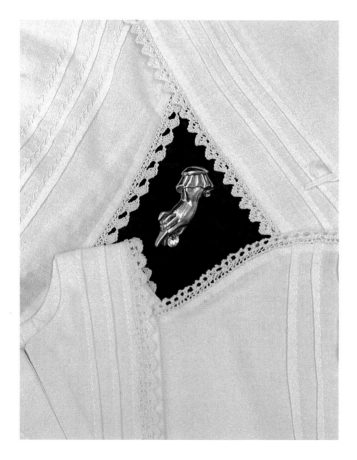

Detail of laces used on Rose White underwear.

14: SERENA

A modern wooden doll 14'' (36 cm).
Her double skirt is knitted in DMC 20 Cotton on 1.25 mm (18) needles. Knitting two skirts eliminates the need for petticoats. The long-line bodice was made from Gunson the Sailor's undervest pattern (see page 76). Over the bodice is a dainty lace jacket. The bouquet is knitted. The outfit requires approximately 7 × 20 g balls of DMC 20 Cotton, plus a small quantity of DMC 100 Cotton for the flowers. Tiny silk ribbons for the bouquet and a small piece of knitted lace to tuck into the corded headdress. A veil of fine tulle or net.
Doll from author's collection.

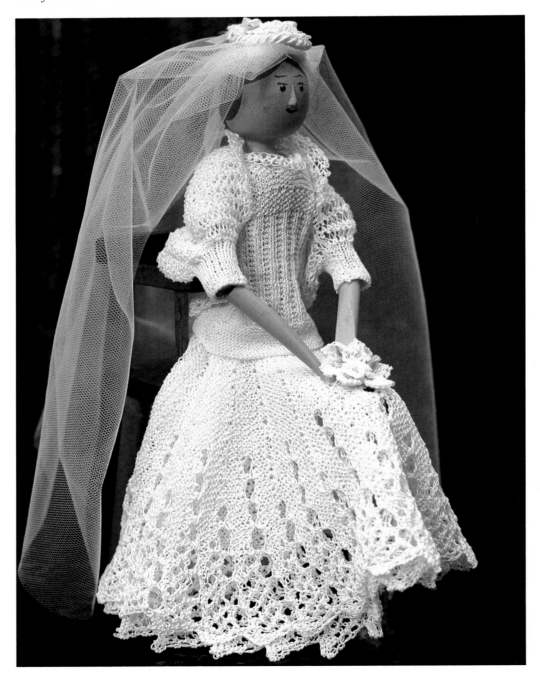

LACE JACKET

Cast on 36 sts.
Work in k1, p1, rib for 1'' (2.25 cm).
Next Row: K7, k twice in next 22 sts, k7 (58 sts).
Continue as follows:
Rows 1 and 2: Knit.
Row 3: K1, * m1, k1, repeat from * to end of row.
Row 4: K1, * drop the next st (which was the m1 of previous row), k1, repeat from * to end of row.
Repeat these 4 rows until length required.

Work cuff:
K7, (k2 tog) to last 7 sts, k7.
Work in k1, p1, rib for 1'' (2.25 cm).
Cast off.

Make up

Join cuffs together. Turn back top of jacket to form collar. A row of dc can be worked around jacket if desired. Use ribbon ties if desired.

SKIRT

Cast on 57 sts.
Row 1: Sl 1, k41, (m1, k2 tog) 7 times, m1, k1.
Row 2: Sl 1, k54, turn (leaving 3 sts).
Row 3: Sl 1, k41, (m1, k2 tog) 6 times, m1, k1.
Row 4: Sl 1, k52, turn (leaving 6 sts).
Row 5: Sl 1, k41 (m1, k2 tog) 5 times, m1, k1.
Row 6: Sl 1, k50, turn (leaving 9 sts).
Row 7: Sl 1, k49, m1, k1.
Row 8: Sl 1, k48, turn (leaving 12 sts).
Row 9: Sl 1, k15, * m3, sl 1, k3 tog, psso *, repeat *-* 7 times, k5.
Row 10: Cast off 4 sts, k2, p1, (k3, p1) 6 times, k14, turn (leaving 15 sts).
Row 11: Sl 1, k41.
Row 12: Sl 1, k38, turn (leaving 18 sts).
Row 13: Sl 1, k23, (m1, k2 tog) 7 times, m1, k1.
Row 14: Sl 1, k36, turn (leaving 21 sts).
Row 15: Sl 1, k23, (m1, k2 tog) 6 times, m1, k1.
Row 16: Sl 1, k34, turn (leaving 24 sts).
Row 17: Sl 1, k23, (m1, k2 tog) 5 times, m1, k1.
Row 18: Sl 1, k32, turn (leaving 27 sts).
Row 19: Sl 1, k31, m1, k1.
Row 20: Sl 1, k30, turn (leaving 30 sts).

Row 21: Sl 1, k5, * m3, sl 1, k3 tog, psso *, repeat *-* 5 times, k5.
Row 22: Cast off 4 sts, k2, p1, (k3, p1) 4 times, k4, turn (leaving 33 sts)
Row 23: Sl 1, k23.
Row 24: Sl 1, k56.
Repeat Rows 1-24 18 times.

BOUQUET

Cast on 2 sts using 1.25 mm (18 needles) and DMC 20 Cotton.
Row 1: Knit inc 1 (to inc 1, k in f and b of st).
Row 2: K3.
Row 3: K3, inc 1.
Row 4: K4.
Row 5: K4, inc 1.
Rows 6-9: K5.
Row 10: Cast off 1 st, k3.
Row 11: K4.
Row 12: Cast off 1 st, k2.
Row 13: K3.
Row 14: Cast off 1 st, k1.
Row 15: K2.
Cast off.
Repeat Rows 1-15 5 times.
These 6 pieces form the base of the bouquet.
Stitch together to form a circle, twisting the pieces to form an attractive setting for the flowers.

Flowers (make two)

Using 1 mm (20) needles and DMC 100 Cotton, cast on 10 sts.
Row 1: K1, (m1, k1) to end of row.
Repeat this row twice. Cast off.
Make flower into a tiny rose by lifting the shape into a circle. Attach roses to base with tiny stitches. Make tiny loops of fine silk ribbon for a touch of colour. Embroider a loop as centre of flower. Attach to doll's hand with a silk ribbon. Neaten back of bouquet. Leave 2 strands of No. 20 Cotton to hang from flower base.

Doll's headpiece consists of a circlet of silk cord stitched together with small sts. Cover join with a ribbon bow. A small piece of knitted lace, gathered to form circle, sits inside the circlet of cord. Add veiling as desired.

15: SAMUEL

Antique wooden peg doll with yellow tuck comb 14'' (36 cm).
The wedding suit consists of jacket, undervest, collar, trousers, hat and stockings.
Approximaely 4 × 50 g balls Missoni Lipari. Small amount of DMC 100 Cotton for the knitted buttonhole. Worked on 2.75 mm (12) needles. For the pattern for the stockings see page 66.
Doll from author's collection.

JACKET

Cast on 46 sts.
Knit 3 rows.
Purl 3 rows.

All shapings are made at neck edge, the other side is the bottom of the jacket which should be straight and even. At end of 14th row inc for shoulder by (k1, p1) in last st, and also at end of 16th, 18th and 20th rows (50 sts). At end of 22nd row begin slope of shoulder by knitting last 2 sts tog.
Continue the slope in each of the 9 following rows (40 sts). At the 41st row cast off 14 sts for armhole, p to end of row (26 sts). Work 8 rows in pattern. At end of 50th row cast on 14 sts for other side of armhole, inc 1 at end of each of next 10 even-numbered rows. Then dec at end of each of next 4 even-numbered rows (46 sts). Work 25 rows for back.
Next Row: Work the inc of shoulder as for Row 14. Shape shoulder and armhole to correspond with previous one. Work same number of ridges on second front as on first. Cast off jacket edging.
With right side facing, pick up 46 sts down left front, 3 sts at corner, 2 sts on each ridge along bottom, 3 sts at corner, 46 sts up other front. Knit 1 row.
Next Row: Beginning at left front, knit to corner, and there inc 2 or 3 sts, knit along bottom of jacket to other corner, inc 2 or 3 sts, k16 sts up the right front, m1, k2 tog, k9, m1, k2 tog, k9, m1, k2 tog, k to end.
Knit 2 rows. Cast off (picot).

Neck edge

Pick up along neck corner to corner of front edges. Knit 4 rows. Cast off (picot).

Sleeves

Cast on 16 sts. Work in ridged pattern, inc 1 at end of 4th row, and at the end of every alternate row until 24 sts on needle. Work 11 rows on the 24 sts, then dec at end of each alternate row until 16 sts remain. When you have worked 46 rows cast off. Pick up and knit 24 sts along sleeve end. Knit 1 row, purl 1 row, knit 1 row. Cast off in picot. Make other sleeve the same way. Sew sleeve seams, sew into armholes. A contrasting edge may be used if desired. Make buttonholes in left front for male doll; sew on buttons. Picot cast off may be omitted if preferred.

UNDERVEST

Cast on 32 sts.
Knit 30 rows.
Cast on 14 sts at beginning of next 2 rows for sleeves.
Knit 19 rows.

Shape neck:
Row 1 (wrong side): K25, cast off 10 sts, k to end of row.
Continue on last 25 sts (leave remaining sts on holder).
Knit 14 rows.
Next Row: Knit.
Shape back of neck:
Cast on 5 sts, k to end of row (30 sts).
Knit 20 rows.
Next Row: Cast off 14 sts for sleeve, k to end of row (16 sts)
Leave sts on holder.
Return to remaining 25 sts. Work other side to correspond.
Next Row: Knit (32 sts).
Knit 30 rows.
Cast off.
Join side and sleeve seams. Make 2 button loops along back opening. Sew on tiny buttons.

Collar

With small needles and 20 g DMC 20 Cotton, knit sailor collar (see page 76). Collar is worn tucked into undervest, lifted to frame the face. A loose bow is tied under chin. Use narrow braid or cord for the tie.

Flower

Using DMC 100 Cotton and 1 mm (20) needles, cast on 10 sts.
Row 1: K1, * m1, k1 *, repeat *-* to end of row.
Repeat Row 1 twice. Cast off.
Arrange to form a tiny rose. Stitch to jacket with fine green thread. Form 3 tiny loops around flower, and use a fine thread for a stem.

TROUSERS

Cast on 26 sts. Work 6'' (15 cm) in st st, ending with purl row.
Leave sts on spare needle.
Work another leg in the same way, ending with a knit row.
Knit the 1st leg on to the same needle (52 sts) and continue in st st.

Dec each end of every 4th row until 40 sts remain.
Next Row: * P2, p2 tog, repeat from * to end of row.
Work 2 rows k1, p1, rib.
Next Row: * Rib 1, m1, k2 tog, repeat from * to end of row.
Work 2 rows k1, p1, rib.
Cast off.

Make up

Press lightly. Sew up trouser seams. Thread elastic or tape through holes at waist.

HAT

Using set of 4 double-pointed needles, cast on 16 sts on each of 2 needles and 18 sts on 3rd needle (50 sts). Work in rounds.

Knit 6 rounds.
Round 7: (M1, k1) to end of round (100 sts).
Knit 6 rounds.
Round 14: (M1, sl 1, k1, psso) to end of round.
Knit 6 rounds.
Round 21: (Sl 1, k1, psso) to end of round (50 sts).
Knit 20 rounds.
Round 42: (M1, sl 1, k1, psso) to end of round.
Knit 2 rounds.
Round 45: (Sl 1, k1, psso, k5) to end of round.
Round 46: (Sl 1, k1, psso, k4) to end of round.
Round 47: (Sl 1, k1, psso, k3) to end of round.
Round 48: (Sl 1, k1, psso, k2) to end of round.
Round 49: (Sl 1, k1, psso, k1) to end of round.
Round 50: (Sl 1, k1, psso) to end of round.

Break off yarn and thread through remaining sts, drawing them together. Fasten off. Turn brim under at 2nd row of holes and hem neatly. Trim hat with narrow ribbon and tiny buckle.

16: MOUNTAIN ASH BED

The bed was crafted by Flick Evans from the wood of Eucalyptus regnans to a scale of 1 to 5½ from an early Australian bed, circa 1840. Measurements 15½'' × 11½'' × 15'' (40 × 29.50 × 38 cm). The bedcover was knitted in 4-ply cotton on 2 mm (14) needles. Quantity of cotton will depend on bed size. The doona and valance (Turkish Delight) were also knitted in 4-ply cotton. The continental pillows are also found in Heirloom Knitting for Dolls.
Bed from author's collection.

BEDCOVER

Cast on 8 sts—3 sts on 1st and 2nd needles, 2 sts on 3rd needle. Work with 4th needle.

Round 1: (M1, k1) 8 times.
Round 2 and all even rounds: Knit.
Round 3: (M1, k2) 8 times.
Round 5: (M1, k3) 8 times.
Round 7: (M1, k4) 8 times.
Round 9: (M1, k5) 8 times.
Round 11: (M1, k1, m1, k2 tog, k3) 8 times.
Round 13: (M1, k3, m1, k2 tog, k2) 8 times.
Round 15: (M1, k5, m1, k2 tog, k1) 8 times.
Round 17: (M1, k7, m1, k2 tog) 8 times.
Round 19: (M1, k1, m1, k2 tog, k5, k2 tog) 8 times.
Round 21: (M1, k1, m1, k2 tog, m1, k2 tog, k5) 8 times.
Round 23: * M1, k1, (m1, k2 tog) 3 times, k4 *, repeat *-* to end of round.
Round 25: * M1, k1, (m1, k2 tog) 4 times, k3 *, repeat *-* to end of round.
Round 27: * M1, k1, (m1, k2 tog) 5 times, k2 *, repeat *-* to end of round.
Round 29: * M1, k1, (m1, k2 tog) 6 times, k1 *, repeat *-* to end of round.
Round 31: * M1, k1, (m1, k2 tog) 7 times *, repeat *-* to end of round.
Rounds 32-34: Knit.

Work welted corner:
Row 1: P30, p2 tog, turn.
Row 2: K29, k2 tog, turn.
Row 3: P28, p2 tog, turn.
Row 4: P to last 2 sts, p2 tog, turn.
Row 5: K to last 2 sts, k2 tog, turn.
Row 6: P to last 2 sts, p2 tog, turn.
Repeat Rows 4-6 until 2 sts remain. Cast off. This completes 1st corner. Place next 32 sts on needle for 2nd corner.
Work as for 1st corner, Continue working in this manner until you have completed 4 corners. This forms the square, repeat until you have sufficient for your project.

The mountain ash bed is trimmed with a simple edging:
Cast on 12 sts.
Row 1: Knit.
Row 2: P9, turn, k9.
Row 3: P9, k3.
Row 4: K3, p9.
Row 5: K9, turn, p9.
Row 6: Knit.
Repeat Rows 1-6 until length required. Sew squares together. Attach edging around bed cover allowing fullness at corners.

DOONA

Cast on 83 sts.
Row 1: P6, * m1, k1, m1, p6, repeat from * to end of row.
Row 2: K6, * p3, k6, repeat from * to end of row.
Row 3: P6, * k1, m1, k1, m1, k1, p6, repeat from * to end of row.
Row 4: K6, * p5, k6, repeat from * to end of row.
Row 5: P6, * k2, m1, k1, m1, k2, p6, repeat from * to end of row.
Row 6: K6, * p7, k6, repeat from * to end of row.
Row 7: P6, * k3, m1, k1, m1, k3, p6, repeat from * to end of row.
Row 8: K6, * p9, k6, repeat from * to end of row.
Row 9: P6, * sl 1, k1, psso, k5, k2 tog, p6, repeat from * to end of row.
Row 10: As Row 6.
Row 11: P6, * sl 1, k1, psso, k3, k2 tog, p6, repeat from * to end of row.
Row 12: As Row 4.
Row 13: P6, * sl 1, k1, psso, k1, k2 tog, p6, repeat from * to end of row.
Row 14: As Row 2.
Row 15: P6, * sl 1, k2 tog, psso, p6, repeat from * to end of row.
Row 16: Knit.
Row 17: Purl.
Repeat last 2 rows.
Row 20: Purl.
Repeat Rows 1-20 7 times.

Edging

Cast on 8 sts.
Row 1 and alternate rows: Knit.
Row 2: Sl 1, k2, (m1, k2 tog) twice, k in f and b of last st (inc 1).
Row 4: Sl 1, k2, m1, k2 tog, k1, m1, k2 tog, inc 1.
Row 6: Sl 1, k2, m1, k2 tog, k2, m1, k2 tog, inc 1.
Row 8: Sl 1, k2, m1, k2 tog, k3, m1, k2 tog, inc 1.
Row 9: Cast off 4 sts, k7.
Repeat Rows 2-9 until length desired. Attach edging to doona cover with tiny sts, allowing fullness at corners. Make a fabric backing for doona. Sl st to knitted cover.

CONTINENTAL PILLOWS

Cast on 1 st and k1, p1, k1 into this st.
Row 1: (M1, k1) 3 times.
Row 2: M1, k1, p3, k2.
Row 3: M1, k3, m1, k1, m1, k3.
Row 4: M1, k2, p5, k3.

Row 5: M1, k5, m1, k1, m1, k5.
Row 6: M1, k3, p7, k4.
Row 7: M1, k7, m1, k1, m1, k7.
Row 8: M1, k4, p9, k5.
Row 9: M1, k9, m1, k1, m1, k9.
Row 10: M1, k5, p11, k6.
Row 11: M1, k11, m1, k1, m1, k11.
Row 12: M1, k6, p13, k7.
Row 13: M1, k13, m1, k1, m1, k13.
Row 14: M1, k7, p15, k8.
Row 15: M1, k8, k2 tog, k11, sl 1, k1, psso, k8.
Row 16: M1, k8, p13, k9.
Row 17: M1, k9, k2 tog, k9, sl 1, k1, psso, k9.
Row 18: M1, k9, p11, k10.
Row 19: M1, k10, k2 tog, k7, sl 1, k1, psso, k10.
Row 20: M1, k10, p9, k11.
Row 21: M1, k11, k2 tog, k5, sl 1, k1, psso, k11.
Row 22: M1, k11, p7, k12.
Row 23: M1, k12, k2 tog, k3, sl 1, k1, psso, k12.
Row 24: M1, k12, p5, k13.
Row 25: M1, k13, k2 tog, k1, sl 1, k1, psso, k13.
Row 26: M1, k13, p3, k14.
Row 27: M1, k14, sl 1, k2 tog, psso, k14.
Row 28: M1, p30.
Row 29: M1, k2 tog, k1, *(m1, k1) twice, sl 1, k1, psso, k1, k2 tog, k1 *, repeat *-* twice, m1, k1, m1, k2 tog, k1.
Row 30: M1, p32.
Row 31: M1, k2 tog, k1, *m1, k3, m1, k1, sl 1, k2 tog, psso, k1 *, repeat *-* twice, m1, k3, m1, k2 tog, k1.
Row 32: M1, p34.
Row 33: M1, k4, k2 tog, k1, m1, k1, *m1, k1, sl 1, k1, psso, k1, k2 tog, k1, m1, k1, *, repeat *-* twice, m1, k2 tog, k1.
Row 34: M1, p36.
Row 35: M1, k2, *m1, k1, sl 1, k2 tog, psso, k1, m1, k3*, repeat *-* 3 times, m1, k2 tog, k1.
Row 36: M1, p38.
Row 37: M1, k4, k2 tog, k1, *(m1, k1) twice, sl 1, k1, psso, k1, k2 tog, k1 *, repeat *-* twice, (m1, k1) twice, sl 1, k1, psso, k4.
Row 38: M1, p40.
Row 39: M1, k4, k2 tog, k1, *m1, k3, m1, k1, sl 1, k2 tog, psso, k1 *, repeat *-* twice, m1, k3, m1, k1, sl 1, k2 tog, psso, k3.
Row 40: M1, p41.
Row 41: M1, p42.
Row 42: M1, k43.
Row 43: M1, p44.
Cast off.
Rows 1-43 form one section of pillow. Repeat 3 times.
Join together to form square.

The tiny pillows are edged with fancy lace, worked thus:
Cast on 4 sts.
Row 1: Sl 1, k1, m2, k2.
Row 2: K3, p1, k2.
Row 3: Sl 1, k5.
Row 4: K6.
Row 5: Sl 1, k1, m2, k2 tog, m2, k2.
Row 6: K3, (p1, k2) twice.
Row 7: Sl 1, k8.
Row 8: Cast off 5 sts, k3.
Repeat Rows 1-8 until the lace is long enough to go around the square, with ample fullness at corners.
Make pillow insert approx. 3'' (8 cm) square. Attach knitting with tiny sts or, if preferred, use the knitted square as a pillow sham. The continental pillows can be filled with lavender or potpourri to keep the doll's bedding fragrant and free from moths.

TURKISH DELIGHT VALANCE

Cast on 16 sts.
Row 1: Knit.
Row 2: K3, m1, k2 tog, (m2, k2 tog) 5 times, k1.
Row 3: K3, (p1, k2) 5 times, m1, k2 tog, k1.
Row 4: K3, m1, k2 tog, k16.
Row 5: K18, m1, k2 tog, k1.
Row 6: K3, m1, k2 tog, m2, k2 tog, cast off 9 sts thus: K1, return the k1 to L.H. needle, drawing 9 sts over without knitting them. Cast on 7 sts on R.H. needle, k2 tog, m2, k2 tog, k1.
Row 7: K3, p10, k1, p1, k2, m1, k2 tog, k1.
Row 8: K3, m1, k2 tog, k15.
Row 9: Cast off 4 sts, k12, m1, k2 tog, k1.
Repeat Rows 2-9 until length desired.

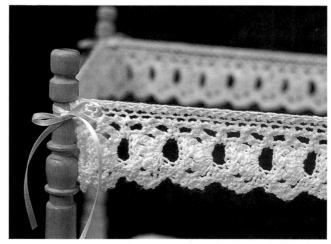

Detail of valance.

17: JEMIMA *(pattern on page 56)*

Antique A.M. 370 16'' (40 cm).
Doll is wearing a full-length lace gown embroidered with delicate rosebuds. Approximately 6 × 20 g balls. DMC Size 20 Cotton, 2.75 mm (12) needles.
Doll from James Botham collection.

18: CELESTINE (pattern on page 57)

Antique S.F.B.J. 60 doll 21'' (54 cm).
A basic black dress knitted on 3 mm (11) needles. Use 2 mm (14) for ribbing at neck. For the dress approximately 6 × 50 g balls of Missoni Lipari. The hemline is knitted in loop st on 3 mm (11) needles with 2 balls of Missoni Lipari. Black buttons. Black and white boa knitted in Anny Blatt Bombay 3 × 50 g balls, worked on 3.75 mm (9) needles. For boa see Pattern 4.
Doll from Blyth collection.

JEMIMA (*illustrated on page 54*)

Cast on 253 sts. Knit 1 row.
Row 1: K2, m1, k3, * sl 1, k2 tog, psso, k3, m1, k1, m1, k3, repeat from * to last 8 sts, sl 1, k2 tog, psso, k3, m1, k2.
Row 2 and alternate rows: K1, purl to last st, k1.
Row 3: * K3, m1, k2, sl 1, k2 tog, psso, k2, m1, repeat from * to last 3 sts, k3.
Row 5: K1, k2 tog, (m1, k1) twice, * sl 1, k2 tog, psso, (k1, m1) twice, sl 1, k2 tog, psso, (m1, k1) twice, repeat from * to last 8 sts, sl 1, k2 tog, psso, (k1, m1) twice, k2 tog, k1.
Row 7: (K1, m1) twice, sl 1, k2 tog, psso, m1, * sl 1, k2 tog, psso, (m1, k1) twice, sl 1, k2 tog, psso, (k1, m1) twice, repeat from * to last 8 sts, (sl 1, k2 tog, psso, m1) twice, k1, m1, k1.
Row 8: As Row 2.
Row 9: Purl.
Row 10: Knit.
Work 6 rows st st, then 2 rows garter st. Inc 5 sts at intervals in last row (258 sts).

Continue in pattern thus:
Row 1: K1, * k2, m1, k2 tog, k4, m1, k2 tog, k2, k2 tog, m1, k2, repeat from * to last st, k1.
Row 2: K1, * (p3, m1, p2 tog) twice, p1, p2 tog, m1, p3, repeat from * to last st, k1.
Row 3: K1, * m1, k2 tog, k2, m1, k2 tog, k4, k2 tog, m1, k4, repeat from * to last st, k1.
Row 4: K1, * m1, p2 tog, p3, m1, p2 tog, p2, p2 tog, m1, p5, repeat from * to last st, k1.
Row 5: K1, * m1, k2 tog, k4, m1, (k2 tog) twice, m1, k6, repeat from * to last st, k1.
Row 6: K1, * m1, p2 tog, p2, p2 tog, m1, p4, m1, p2 tog, p4, repeat from * to last st, k1.
Row 7: K1, * m1, k2 tog, k1, k2 tog, m1, k6, m1, k2 tog, k3, repeat from * to last st, k1.
Row 8: K1, * p2, p2 tog, m1, p4, (m1, p2 tog, p2) twice, repeat from * to last st, k1.
Row 9: K1, * k1, k2 tog, m1, k5, m1, k2 tog, k3, m1, k2 tog, k1, repeat from * to last st, k1.
Row 10: K1, * p2 tog, m1, p6, m1, p2 tog, p4, m1, p2 tog, repeat from * to last st, k1.
Repeat Rows 1–10 6 times.
Dec for waist:
K2 (k2 tog) to end of row.

Work 5 rows in k2, p2, rib.
Ribbon holes:
* K2, m1, k2 tog, repeat from * to end of row.
Work 5 rows in k2, p2, rib.

Change to 2 mm (14) needles.
Row 1: K2, (p1, k1, p1, k2) to last 3 sts, p1, k1, p1.
Row 2: P3, (k1, p4), repeat to last 2 sts, k2.
Repeat last 2 rows 24 times.
Divide for left back:
K35, turn. Work 29 rows in rib pattern.
At armhole edge work 8 rows in st st on 9 sts.
Cast off these 9 sts, leaving 26 sts on spare needle.
Knit 60 sts at centre, turn. Work 29 rows in rib pattern.
At armhole edges work 8 rows in st st on 9 sts. Cast off, leaving centre sts on spare needle.
Work right side to match.

Sleeves

Using 2 mm (14) needles, cast on 53 sts.
Work 8 rows of pattern at bottom of skirt.
Work 3 rows in k2, p2, rib.
Work row of ribbon holes thus:
* K2, m1, k2 tog, repeat from * to end of row.
Work 3 rows in k2, p2, rib.
Dec 3 sts evenly across row (50 sts).
Continue in rib pattern of bodice for 4'' (10 cm) or length desired.

Make up

Sew shoulder seams.
Pick up and knit sts at neck and shoulders. Knit 4 rows.
Work row of ribbon holes thus:
* K2, m1, k2 tog, repeat from * to end of row.
Knit 4 rows.
Cast off.
Lightly press dress. Insert ribbons through waist, armholes and neck. Dress fastens at back with ribbon ties at neck and waist. Back seam can be closed if desired. Crochet a picot edging around neck and sleeves. Work rosebuds on shoulders and hem if desired.

CELESTINE (*illustrated on page 55*)

DRESS

Cast on 168 sts.
Row 1: K1, * m1, (k2 tog) twice, m1, k4, repeat from * to end of row.
Row 2: Knit.
Continue in skirt pattern until work measures 11'' (28 cm).
Shape waist:
K2 tog across row, decreasing 11 sts evenly.
Work k1, p1, rib for 1'' (2.5 cm).
Next Row: (K1, m1, k2 tog, k1) to end of row.
Work k1, p1, rib for 1'' (2.5 cm).
Knit 2 rows.
With right side of work facing, work in st st for bodice.
Next Row: K57, place next 18 sts on holder, turn, purl 39, place 18 sts on holder.
Work 5 rows st st.
Cast off 2 sts at beginning of next 4 rows.
Work 10 rows st st.

Divide for shoulder:
K11, cast off 9 sts, k11.
Row 1: Purl.
Row 2: Cast off 2 sts, k to end of row.
Row 3: Purl.
Row 4: Cast off 1 st, k to end of row.
Work 3 rows st st.
Cast off.
Knit other shoulder to correspond.

Back

Pick up 18 sts for first half of back.
Work 6 rows st st.
Cast off 2 sts at next and alternate row.
Work 18 rows st st.
Cast off.

Sleeves

Cast on 30 sts.
K1, p1, rib for 1'' (2.5 cm).
Make a row of ribbon holes.
K1, p1, rib for 4 rows.
Next Row: K1, p1 in every st.
Inc evenly 5 times across row (65 sts).
Work in skirt pattern until sleeve measures 6'' (15 cm).

Shape top, keeping pattern correct:
Dec 3 sts at beginning of next 6 rows.
Next Row: (K2 tog) to end of row.
Next Row: (P2 tog) to end of row.
Cast off.

Make up

Press skirt and sleeves lightly. Sew up back seam to ribbon holes. With right side facing pick up and knit 23 sts from each side of back opening (46 sts).
Knit 3 rows.
Next Row: * K4, m1, k2 tog, repeat from * twice (3 buttonholes), k to end of row.
Next Row: Knit.
Cast off.
Sew shoulder seams. With right side of work facing and using 2 mm (14) needles, pick up and knit 38 sts.
Work 2 rows k1, p1, rib.
Next Row: Make buttonhole on same level as others.
Work 2 rows k1, p1, rib.
Cast off.
Sew sleeves into armholes. Sew up side and sleeve seams. Sew on buttons. Thread ribbons through holes at waist and wrists.

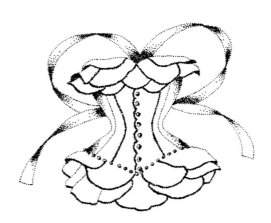

19: BENJAMIN

Reproduction doll by Thea Moore 8'' (20 cm).
Clothes designed and knitted by Thea in 3-py Cotton on 2 mm (14) needles.
Doll from David Moore collection.

JACKET

Jacket is worked in one piece starting at centre back. Cast on 40 sts.

Rows 1 and 2: Knit.
Rows 3-6: K30, turn.
Rows 7 and 8: K40.
Repeat Rows 3-8 6 times.

Row 45: K40.
Row 46: K10, place remaining sts on holder.

Sleeve

Cast on 20 sts (30 sts).
Row 1: Knit.

Row 2: * K25, turn (cuff).
Row 3: K15, turn.
Rows 4 and 5: K20, turn.
Row 6: K15, turn.
Row 7: K25, turn.
Row 8: K30, turn.
Row 9: K20, turn.
Rows 10 and 11: K15, turn.
Row 12: K20, turn.
Repeat from * once.
Next Row: K30.
Repeat this row once.
Cast off 20 sts (completes 1st sleeve).
K10.
K10, add sts from holder.
K40.
Repeat Rows 3-8 14 times for front.
K40.
K10, place remaining 30 sts on holder.
Repeat sleeve section.
Work other side of back.
End with buttonhole row worked thus:
K2, m1, k2 tog, * k4, m1, k2 tog, repeat from * 4 times, k6.
Cast off.
Press lightly. Thread ribbon through yoke. Sew on buttons or tiny beads. Work 3 rosebuds on front of yoke.

LEGGINGS

Cast on 30 sts.
Row 1: Knit.
Row 2: * P1, m1, p2 tog, repeat from * to last st, p1.
Row 3: Knit.
Row 4: Purl.
Repeat Rows 3-4 7 times.

Row 19: Inc each end of needle, knit.
Row 20: Purl.
Repeat Rows 19-20 3 times.
Row 27: Dec each end of needle, knit.
Row 28: Purl.
Repeat Rows 27-28 6 times.
Row 41: Knit.
Row 42: Purl.
Repeat Rows 41-42 14 times.
Row 57: K1, k2 tog, (k8, k2 tog) twice, k1.
Row 58: P10, p2 tog, p9.
Row 59: K1, (k2 tog, k6) twice, k2 tog, k1.
Row 60: P8, p2 tog, p7.
Row 61: K1, k2 tog, (k4, k2 tog) twice, k1.
Row 62: Purl.
Row 63: Knit.
Row 64: Purl.
Cast off. Make other side of leggings. Sew feet, leg and body seams. Thread ribbon or elastic through holes at waist.

BONNET

Cast on 30 sts.
Rows 1 and 2: Knit.
Row 3: K2, p26, k2.
Row 4: Knit.
Repeat rows 3-4 8 times.
Cast off 10 sts on each side.
Work 12 rows in st st.
Knit 2 rows.
Cast off.
Sew back to side section. Sew ribbons to sides. Embroider rosebuds at ribbon ties.

20: TREEN LACE

Black lace knitted on 1 mm (20) needles using DMC 100 Cotton. A length of firm braid worked on 1 mm (20) needles in 20 DMC Cotton. Quantity of yarn will depend on your project. To facilitate working in black thread use light-coloured needles.

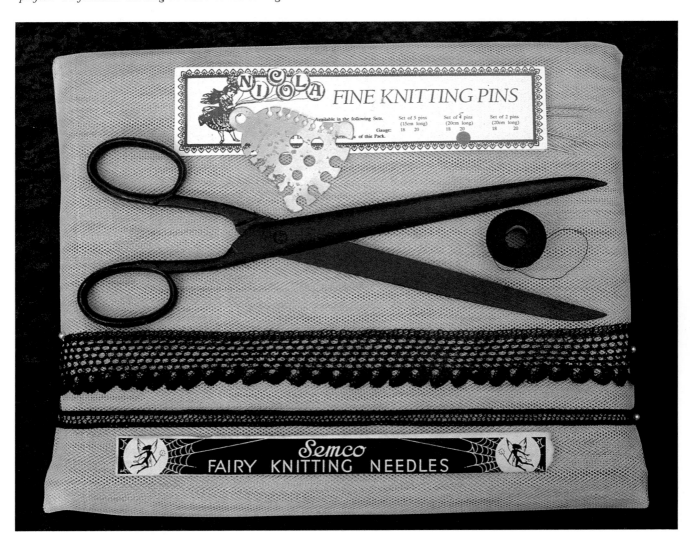

Cast on 17 sts.
Row 1: Sl 1, k3, (m1, k2 tog) 5 times, cast on 4 sts, k2 tog, k1.
Row 2: K20.
Row 3: Sl 1, k13, (k1, p1) in each of next 4 sts, k2.
Row 4: K24.
Row 5: Sl 1, k3, (m1, k2 tog) 5 times, k10.
Row 6: Knit.
Row 7: Knit.
Row 8: Cast off 7 sts, k16.
Repeat Rows 1–8 until length desired.

BLACK BRAID

Cast on 6 sts using DMC 100 Cotton and 1 mm (20) needles.
Row 1: Sl 1, k2, m1, k2 tog, k1.
Repeat this row until length desired.
Cast off.

21: TRIMS

Four different trims to embellish your knitting.

POMPOMS

Cast on 10 sts.
Purl 1 row.
Next Row: Inc k-wise into every st (20 sts).
Beginning with a purl row, work 6 rows st st.
Then (p2 tog) to end of row.
Cut yarn. Join ends. Turn right side out. Stuff pompom with cotton wool. Thread yarn through cast-on sts and pull thread tightly. Fasten off.

BEADED LACE

Using 1 mm (20) needles and DMC 100 Cotton Blanc 5200, cast on 5 sts.
Row 1: Sl 1, k1, m1, k2 tog, k1.
Row 2: As Row 1.
Row 3: As Row 1 to last st, k in f, b, f.
Row 4: Sl 1, k1, psso, k1, pass first st over, k1, m1, k2 tog, k1.
Repeat Rows 1–4 until length desired.

The wider version of beaded lace was knitted on 1.25 mm (18) needles in DMC 20 Cotton Blanc 5200, using 7 sts.
Row 1: Sl 1, k1, (m1, k2 tog) twice, k1.
Row 2: As Row 1.
Row 3: As Row 1 to last st, k in f, b, f.
Row 4: Sl 1, k1, psso, k1, pass first st over, k1, (m1, k2 tog) twice, k1.
Repeat Rows 1–4 until length desired.
An example of how different threads and needles change the appearance of lace edgings.

SEA SHELL TRIM

Cast on 4 sts.
Row 1: * K1, m2, repeat from * to end of row.
Row 2: * P dropping extra loop, repeat from * to end of row.
Row 3: K4 tog.
Row 4: P1.
Row 5: Into 1 st cast on 3 sts.
Repeat Rows 1–5 until length desired.

ARUM LILY

Cast on 144 sts: 36 sts on 4 double-pointed needles. Work with 5th needles. Purl 4 rounds.
Proceed as follows:
Round 5: K1, k2 tog, k to last 3 sts, k2 tog, k1.
Round 6: Knit.
Repeat Rounds 5–6 twice.
Purl 4 rounds.
Dec in this way until 2 sts remain on each needle.
Cast off.
Thread yarn through sts. Fasten off. Fold the square to form the spathe of the lily. Make a length of classic cord (*see* next page) in yellow cotton for the spadix of the lily. Insert spadix and stitch to spathe.

Leaf

Cast on 24 sts. Knit 1 row.
Row 1: K1, sl 1, k1, psso, k to last 3 sts, k2 tog, k1.
Rows 2–4: Knit.
Repeat these 4 rows until 6 sts remain.
Next Row: K1, sl 1, psso, k2 tog, k1.
Next Row: (K2 tog) twice.
Next Row: K2 tog.
Cut thread and draw yarn through remaining stitch.
Arrange lily to your requirements.

Detail of arum lily.

22: TRIMS

Three designs to knit, including the useful cord.

CIRCULAR FLOWER

Cast on 12 sts.
Row 1: Sl 1, k3, (m2, k2 tog) 4 times
Row 2: (K2, p1) 4 times, k4.
Row 3: Sl 1, k15.
Row 4: Cast off 4 sts, k11.
Repeat Rows 1–4 until the work forms a circle. Sew edges together. Wash the flower and dry on towel. Use as desired.

CLASSIC CORD

Cast on 3 sts using double-pointed needle.
Row 1: * K3, do not turn. Slide sts to other side of needle*.
Repeat *–* until length desired.
Cast off.

TURKISH DELIGHT VALANCE

Cast on 16 sts.
Row 1: Knit.
Row 2: K3, m1, k2 tog, (m2, k2 tog) 5 times, k1.
Row 3: K3, (p1, k2) 5 times, m1, k2 tog, k1.
Row 4: K3, m1, k2 tog, k16.
Row 5: K18, m1, k2 tog, k1.
Row 6: K3, m1, k2 tog, m2, k2 tog, cast off 9 sts thus: K1, return the k1 to L.H. needle, drawing 9 sts over without knitting them. Cast on 7 sts on R.H. needle, k2 tog, m2, k2 tog, k1.
Row 7: K3, p10, k1, p1, k2, m1, k2 tog, k1.
Row 8: K3, m1, k2 tog, k15.
Row 9: Cast off 4 sts, k12, m1, k2 tog, k1.
Repeat Rows 2–9 until length desired.

23: SEVEN EDGINGS

A selection of seven edgings. Use yarn and needles of your choice.

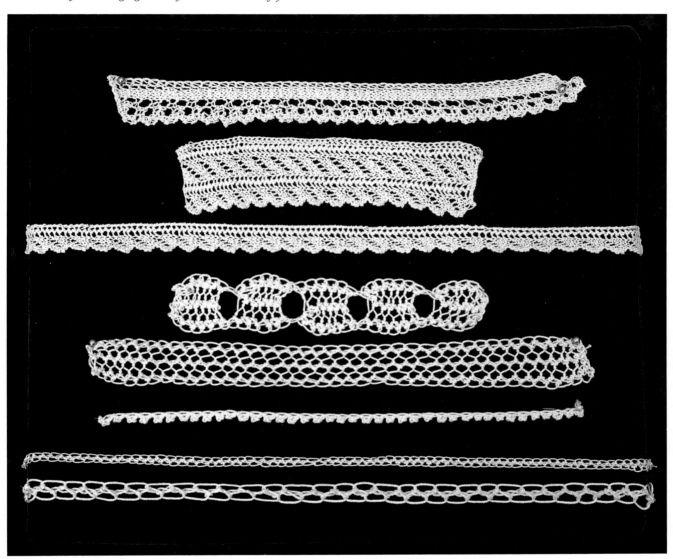

BODKIN LACE

Cast on 9 sts.
Row 1: Sl 1, k1, m1, sl 1, k3, psso over k3 sts, m1, k1, m2, k2.
Row 2: Sl 1, k2, p1, k2, p3, k3.
Row 3: Sl 1, k1, m1, sl 1, k3, psso over k3 sts, k6.
Row 4: Cast off 3 sts, k2, p3, k3.
Repeat Rows 1–4 until length desired.

CANDY LACE

Cast on 15 sts.
Row 1: Sl 1, k1, m1, p2 tog, k1, m1, k2 tog, k3, m1, p2 tog, k1, m1, k2.
Row 2: K2, p1, k1, m1, p2 tog, k4, p1, k1, m1, p2 tog, k2.
Row 3: Sl 1, k1, m1, p2 tog, k2, m1, k2 tog, k2, m1, p2 tog, k2, m1, k2.

Row 4: K2, p1, k2, m1, p2 tog, k3, p1, k2, m1, p2 tog, k2.
Row 5: Sl 1, k1, m1, p2 tog, k3, m1, k2 tog, k1, m1, p2 tog, k3, m1, k2.
Row 6: K2, (p1, k3, m1, p2 tog, k2) twice.
Row 7: Sl 1, k1, m1, p2 tog, k4, m1, k2 tog, m1, p2 tog, k6.
Row 8: Cast off 3 sts, k2, m1, p2 tog, k1, p1, k4, m1, p2 tog, k2.
Repeat Rows 1–8 until length desired.

CANDY EDGING

Cast on 7 sts.
Row 1: Sl 1, k1, m1, p2 tog, k1, m1, k2.
Row 2: K2, p1, k1, m1, p2 tog, k2.
Row 3: Sl 1, k1, m1, p2 tog, k2, m1, k2.
Row 4: K2, p1, k2, m1, p2 tog, k2.
Row 5: Sl 1, k1, m1, p2 tog, k3, m1, k2.
Row 6: K2, p1, k3, m1, p2 tog, k2.
Row 7: Sl 1, k1, m1, p2 tog, k6.
Row 8: Cast off 3 sts, k2, m1, p2 tog, k2.
Repeat Rows 1–8 until length desired.

WINGED BRAID

Cast on 6 sts.
Rows 1–10: (M1, p2 tog) 3 times.
Row 11: M1, sl 1, p3 tog, pass sl st and made st over, m4, p2 tog.
Row 12: M1, sl 1, k1, p1, k1, m1, p2 tog.
Row 13: (M1, p2 tog) twice, m1, p3 tog.
Repeat Rows 1–13 until length desired.

STRAIGHT BRAID

Cast on 6 sts.
Row 1: (M1, p3 tog) 3 times.
Repeat this row until length desired.

PICOT POINT TRIM

Cast on 1 st.
Row 1: Cast on 2 sts.
Row 2: Cast off 2 sts.
Repeat Rows 1 and 2 (without turning the needles) until length desired.

LACE CHAIN

Cast on 2 sts.
Row 1: M1, p2 tog.
Repeat this row until length desired.

24: STOCKINGS, SOCKS & MITTENS

Stockings are knitted in 3-ply cotton on a set of 2.75 mm (12) double-pointed needles. White ribbed sack socks are knitted in 3-ply cotton on a set of 2.75 mm (12) double-pointed needles. Fine black sack socks are knitted in DMC 100 Cotton on a set of 1 mm (20) double-pointed needles. Both sack sock patterns date from the 1880s. White mittens of basic design are worked in 3-ply cotton on 1.25 mm (18) needles.

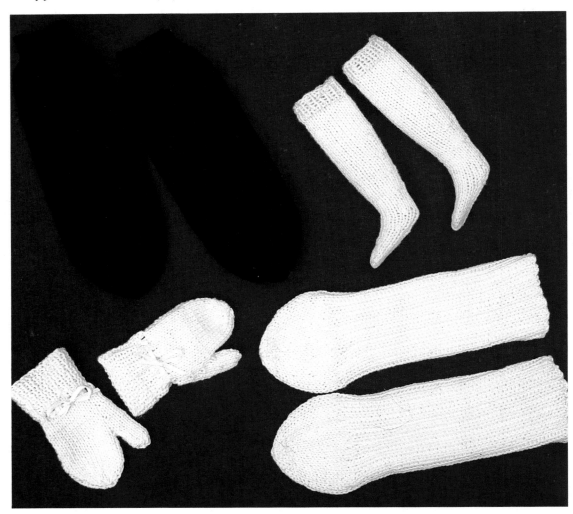

STOCKINGS

Using a set of 4 double-pointed needles cast on 24 sts, 8 sts on each of 3 needles. Work with 4th needle.
Work 5 rounds k1, p1, rib.
Round 6: Knit.
Repeat Round 6 14 times.
Round 21: K1, k2 tog, k to last 2 sts, sl 1, k1, psso.

Round 22: Knit.
Repeat Round 22 4 times.
Repeat Rounds 21–26 5 times.
Round 58: Knit.
Repeat Round 58 4 times.
Round 63: (K2 tog) to end of round.
Round 64: Knit.
Cut thread. Thread through remaining sts. Fasten off.

WHITE SACK SOCKS

Cast on 60 sts, using a set of four double-pointed needles.
Rib k2, p2, until length required.
Shape toe:
Round 1: * K1, k2 tog, k3, repeat from * to end of round.
Knit 5 rounds.
Round 7: * K1, k2 tog, k2, repeat from * to end of round.
Knit 4 rounds.
Round 12: * K1, k2 tog, k1, repeat from * to end of round.
Knit 3 rounds.
Round 16: * K1, k2 tog, repeat from * to end of round.
Knit 2 rounds.
Round 19: K2 tog to end of round.
Round 20: Knit.
Break off yarn. Thread through sewing needle and slip through sts on needles. Pass needle through to wrong side of work, drawing yarn tight to close toe. Fasten off securely.

BLACK SACK SOCKS

Using DMC 100 thread and a set of 4 1.25 mm (18) double-pointed needles, proceed as follows:
Cast on 60 sts (20 sts on each of 3 needles; work with 4th needle).
K2, p2, rib for approx ¾ '' (2 cm). Continue to knit every round until length required.
Shape toe as for white sock.
This is a versatile pattern of the 1880s. By the use of different sts and threads you can create socks to your design, and enhance your doll's appearance, without turning heels. The socks could be worked on 2 needles if you prefer. However, the use of double-pointed needles eliminates the need for seams.

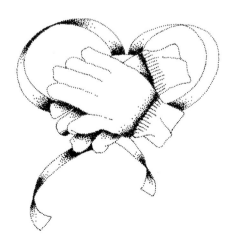

WHITE MITTENS

Cast on 35 sts.
Row 1: (K1, p1) to last st, k1.
Repeat Row 1 15 times.
Row 17: K4, (k2 tog, k3) to last st, k1 (29 sts).
Row 18 and alternate rows: K1, purl to last st, k1.
Row 19: K1, (m1, k2 tog) to end of row.
Row 21: K13, (inc 1 in next st) twice, k14.
Row 23: Knit.
Row 25: K13, inc 1 in next st, k2, inc 1 in next st, k14.
Row 27: Knit.
Row 29: K13, inc 1 in next st, k4, inc 1 in next st, k14.
Row 30: As Row 18.

Thumb

Next Row: K22, turn, cast on 1 st.
Work 6 rows on these sts.
Next Row: K1, * k2 tog, repeat from * to end of the row.
Cut the yarn leaving long thread. With darning needle thread through remaining sts. Draw up and fasten off securely.
With right side facing, join in yarn. Knit up 2 sts from cast on sts at base of thumb, k remaining 13 sts.
Next Row: K1, purl to last st, k1.
Work 8 rows without shaping.

Shape top

Row 1: (K2 tog, k2), repeat to end of row.
Rows 2 and 4: K1, p to last st, k1.
Row 3: (K2 tog, k1) to end of row.
Row 5: (k2 tog), repeat to end of row.
Cut the yarn. Thread end through remaining sts and draw up. Fasten off securely. Sew up thumb and side seams. Thread fine ribbon through holes at wrist. Repeat pattern for 2nd mitten.

25: SIX EDGINGS

Six lace edgings to trim your doll's outfit or underwear.

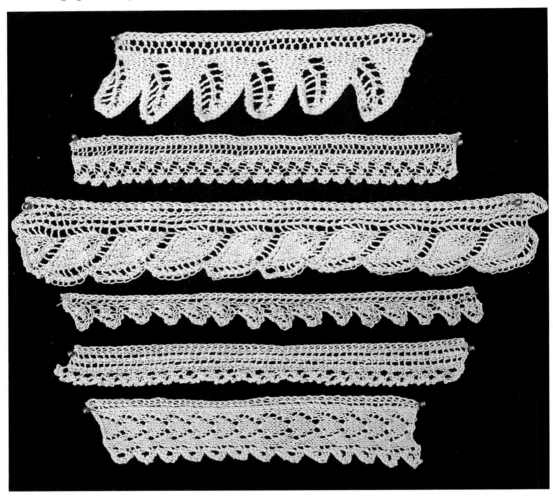

CORONET LEAF

Cast on 11 sts.
Row 1: Sl 1, k2, m1, k2 tog, k1, (m2, k2 tog) twice, k1.
Row 2: Sl 1, (k2, p1) twice, k3, m1, k2 tog, k1.
Row 3: Sl 1, k2, m1, k2 tog, k3, (m2, k2 tog) twice, k1.
Row 4: Sl 1, (k2, p1) twice, k5, m1, k2 tog, k1.
Row 5: Sl 1, k2, m1, k2 tog, k5, (m2, k2 tog) twice, k1.
Row 6: Sl 1, (k2, p1) twice, k7, m1, k2 tog, k1.
Row 7: Sl 1, k2, m1, k2 tog, k7 (m2, k2 tog) twice, k1.
Row 8: Sl 1, (k2, p1) twice, k9, m1, k2 tog, k1.
Row 9: Sl 1, k2, m1, k2 tog, k9, (m2, k2 tog) twice, k1.
Row 10: Sl 1, (k2, p1) twice, k11, m1, k2 tog, k1.
Row 11: Sl 1, k2, m1, k2 tog, k11, (m2, k2 tog) twice, k1.
Row 12: Sl 1, (k2, p1) twice, k13, m1, k2 tog, k1.
Row 13: Sl 1, k2, m1, k2 tog, k18.
Row 14: Cast off 12 sts, k7, m1, k2 tog, k1.
Repeat Rows 1–14 until length desired.

JAUNTY LACE

Cast on 11 sts.
Row 1: K4, m1, p2 tog, k4, m1, (k and p in last st).
Row 2: K3, m1, p2 tog, k4, m1, p2 tog, k2.
Row 3: K4, m1, p2 tog, k1, p2 tog, m1, k4.
Row 4: K5, m1, p2 tog, k2, m1, p2 tog, k2.
Row 5: K4, m1, p2 tog, k2, m1, p2 tog, k3.
Row 6: Cast off 3 sts, m1, k5, m1, p2 tog, k2.
Repeat Rows 1–6 until length desired.

LEAF LACE

Cast on 13 sts.

Row 1: Sl 1, k2 tog (m1, k2 tog) 3 times, m2, k1, m2, k2 tog, k1.
Row 2: M1, p2 tog (k1, p1) in m2 of previous row, k2, p1, k8.
Row 3: Sl 1, k2 tog, (m1, k2 tog) 3 times, m2, k3, m2, k2 tog, k1.
Row 4: M1, p2 tog, (k1, p1) in m2 of previous row, k4, p1, k8.
Row 5: Sl 1, k2 tog, (m1, k2 tog) 3 times, m2, (k1, p1) twice, k1, m2, k2 tog, k1.
Row 6: M1, p2 tog, (k1, p1) in m2 of previous row, k2, p1, k3, p1, k8.
Row 7: Sl 1, k2 tog, (m1, k2 tog) 3 times, m2, k2 tog, p1, m1, k1, m1, p1, k2 tog, m2, k2 tog, k1.
Row 8: M1, p2 tog, (k1, p1) in m2 of previous row, k1, p3, k4, p1, k8.
Row 9: Sl 1, k2 tog, (m1, k2 tog) 3 times, m2, k2 tog, p1, (k1, m1) twice, k1, p1, k2 tog, m2, k2 tog, k1.
Row 10: M1, p2 tog, (k1, p1) in m2 of previous row, k2, p5, k3, p1, k8.
Row 11: Sl 1, k2 tog, (m1, k2 tog) 3 times, m2, k2 tog, p1, k2, m1, k1, m1, k2, p1, k2 tog, m2, k2 tog, k1.
Row 12: M1, p2 tog, p1, k3, p7, k3, p1, k8.
Row 13: Sl 1, k2 tog, (m1, k2 tog) 3 times, m2, k2 tog, p1, k7, p1, k2 tog, m2, k2 tog, k1.
Row 14: M1, p2 tog, p1, k3, p7, k3, (p1, k1) in same st, k8.
Row 15: Sl 1, k2 tog, (m1, k2 tog) 3 times, m2, k1, m2, k2 tog, p1, k7, p1, k2 tog, m2, k2 tog, k1.
Row 16: M1, p2 tog, (k1, p1) in m2 of previous row, k2, p7, k3, p1, k2, p1, k8.
Row 17: Sl 1, k2 tog, (m1, k2 tog) 3 times, m2, k3, m2, k2 tog, p1, k2 tog, k3, k2 tog, p1, k2 tog, m2, k2 tog, k1.
Row 18: M1, p2 tog, (k1, p1) in m2 of previous row, k2, p5, k3, p1, k4, p1, k8.
Row 19: Sl 1, k2 tog, (m1, k2 tog) 3 times, m2, (k1, p1) twice, k1, m2, k2 tog, p1, k2 tog, k1, k2 tog, p1, k2 tog, m2, k2 tog, k1.
Row 20: M1, p2 tog, (k1, p1) in m2 of previous row, k2, p3, k3, p1, k2, p1, k3, p1, k8.
Row 21: Sl 1, k2 tog, (m1, k2 tog) 3 times, m2, k2 tog, p1, m1, k1, m1, p1, k2 tog, m2, k2 tog, p1, k2 tog, k1, p1, k2 tog, m2, k2 tog, k1.
Row 22: M1, p2 tog, (k1, p1) in m2 of previous row, k2, p2 tog, k3, p2, k1, p3, k3, p1, k8.
Row 23: Sl 1, k2 tog, (m1, k2 tog) 3 times, m2, k2 tog, p1, k1, (m1, k1) twice, p1, k2 tog, m2, k2 tog, p3 tog, k2 tog, m2, k2 tog, k1.
Row 24: M1, p2 tog, (k1, p1) in m2 of previous row, k4, p1, k2, p5, k3, p1, k8.
Row 25: Sl 1, k2 tog, (m1, k2 tog) 3 times, m2, k2 tog, p1, k2, m1, k1, m1, k2, p1, (k2 tog, m2, k2 tog, k1) twice.
Row 26: M1, p2 tog, (k1, p1) in m2 of previous row, k3 tog, p1, k3, p7, k3, p1, k8.
Row 27: Sl 1, k2 tog, (m1, k2 tog) 3 times, m2, k2 tog, p1, k7, p1, k2 tog, m2, k2 tog, k4.
Row 28: Cast off 4 sts, k1, p1, m1, k2, p7, k2, m1, k1, p1, k8.
Repeat from Row 15 until length desired.

HAWTHORN LACE

Cast on 6 sts.

Row 1: Sl 1, k3, m1, k2.
Row 2: K2, (m1, k1) twice, m1, k2 tog, k1.
Row 3: Sl 1, k3, m1, k3, m1, k2.
Row 4: K2, m1, k5, m1, k1, m1, k2 tog, k1.
Row 5: Sl 1, k3, m1, k2 tog, k3, k2 tog, m1, k2.
Row 6: K3, m1, k2 tog, k1, k2 tog, m1, k2, m1, k2 tog, k1.
Row 7: Sl 1, k5, m1, sl 1, k2 tog, psso, m1, k4.
Row 8: Cast off 7 sts, k2, m1, k2 tog, k1.
Repeat Rows 1–8 until length desired.

CELANDINE

Cast on 11 sts.

Row 1: K3, (m1, sl 1, k1, psso, k1) twice, (m2, k1) twice.
Row 2: (K2, p1) 4 times, k3.
Row 3: K3, m1, sl 1, k1, psso, k1, m1, sl 1, k1, psso, k7.
Row 4: Cast off 4 sts, k4, p1, k1, p1, k3.
Repeat Rows 1–4 until length desired.

OLIVIA LACE

Cast on 16 sts.
Work a foundation row thus:
K2, p11, k3.
Row 1: Sl 1, k1, m1, k2 tog, k3, m1, sl 1, k2 tog, psso, m1, k4, m1, k2.
Row 2: K3, p11, k3.
Row 3: Sl 1, k1, m1, k2 tog, k1, k2 tog, m1, k3, m1, sl 1, k1, psso, k2, m1, k3.
Row 4: K3, p12, k3.
Row 5: Sl 1, k1, m1, (k2 tog) twice, m1, k5, m1, sl 1, k1, psso, k1, m1, k2 tog, m3, k2.
Row 6: K2, (k1, p1, k1 in m3 of previous row), k2, p11, k3.
Row 7: Sl 1, k1, m1, k2 tog, k1, m1, sl 1, k1, psso, k3, k2 tog, m1, k2, m1, k7.
Row 8: Cast off 6 sts, k1, p11, k3.
Repeat Rows 1–8 until length desired.

26: FRITH

Antique Jumeau doll 21'' (53 cm).
The black and white winter coat was knitted on 4 mm (8) needles, using approximately 4
balls of Pinqouin Cottage yarn. The red bonnet and mittens require 2 balls of Anny Blatt
Coton d'Egypt (8 ply) and 3.25 mm (10) needles.
Doll from Pat Blyth collection.

COAT

Back

Cast on 60 sts using 4 mm (8) needles. Knit 4 rows. Work in st st for 3'' (7.50 cm), then dec 1 st each end on next and following 8th row until 52 sts on needle.
Work until back measures 9'' (23 cm), ending on purl row.
Shape raglan:
Cast off 6 sts at beginning of next 2 rows.
Continue thus:
Row 1: K1, sl 1, k1, psso, knit to last 3 sts, k2 tog, k1.
Row 2: K1, purl to last st, k1.
Repeat last 2 rows until 13 sts remain.
Work 3 rows without shaping. Cast off.

Left front

Cast on 30 sts. Knit 4 rows, increasing 1 st at end of last row (side edge).
Row 1: Knit.
Row 2: K7, purl to end.
Repeat last 2 rows, decreasing at side edge as for back until 26 sts remain. Continue without shaping until work measures 9'' (23 cm) ending at side edge.
Shape raglan:
Cast off 2 sts at beginning of next row.
Row 1: Work to last st, k1.
Row 2: K1, sl 1, k1, psso, work to end.
Repeat Rows 1–2 until 17 sts remain ending at front edge.
Shape neck:
Cast off 8 sts once, then 3 sts once, on alternate rows; at the same time continue raglan shaping until 2 sts remain. Fasten off.

Right front

As for left front in reverse. Make a buttonhole in the 6th row after start of raglan shaping. Work raglan shaping by k2 tog.

Sleeves

Cast on 30 sts. Knit 4 rows.
Continue in st st, increasing 1 st each end of next and following 6th row until 40 sts on needle.
Continue until sleeve measures 6'' (15 cm).
Shape raglan:
Work as for back until 7 sts remain. Work 3 rows without shaping.
Cast off.

Collar

Cast on 68 sts. Knit 4 rows.
Row 1: Knit.
Row 2: K4, purl to last 4 sts, k4.
Repeat last 2 rows until work measures 2¼'' (6 cm) ending on wrong side.
Next Row: K5, * k2 tog, k2, repeat from * to last 4 sts, k4.
Work 4 rows.
Cast off.

Make up

Press lightly. Sew raglan seams, then side and sleeve seams. Sew on collar 10 sts from front edges. Sew on buttons. Buttonholes can be worked on lefthand side for boy doll.

BONNET

Cast on 54 sts.
Work 4 rows k1, p1, rib.
Work 20 rows in st st, starting with k row.
Cast off 16 sts at beginning of next 2 rows.
Work 22 rows in st st on the remaining 22 sts.
Cast off.
Sew bonnet seams:
Pick up and knit 54 sts around neck edge of bonnet.
Work in k1, p1, rib for 4 rows.
Work a row of ribbon holes thus:
(K2, m1, k2 tog) to end of row.
Work 5 rows in k1, p1, rib.
Cast off.
Press bonnet. Thread cord or ribbon through holes and tie under chin.

MITTENS

Cast on 24 sts.
Work in k1, p1, rib for 4 rows.
Work a row of ribbon holes thus:
(K2, m1, k2 tog) to end of row.
Work 2 more rows in rib, increasing 5 sts evenly on last row (29 sts).
Continue in moss st for 13 rows.
Next Row: K1, (k3 tog, p1) 6 times, k3 tog, k1 (15 sts).
Break off yarn and thread through remaining sts, drawing them up. Sew up side seam. Thread ribbon or cord through holes.

27: COATHANGERS

Three coathangers with matching lavender bags designed and made for this book by Joan Eckersley. Use 1.50 mm (16) needles and DMC No. 10 Cotton. A perfect gift for a doll collector.

KENT

Coathanger

Cast on 26 sts. Knit 1 row.
Row 1: Sl 1, k2, m1, (k2 tog) twice, m2, sl 1, k1, psso, k3, m1, (k2 tog) twice, m2, sl 1, k1, psso, k4, m1, k2 tog, m1, k2 (27 sts).
Row 2: M1, k2 tog, k9, p1, k8, p1, k6.
Row 3: Sl 1, k20, (m1, k2 tog) twice, m1, k2.
Row 4: M1, k2 tog, k26.
Row 5: Sl 1, k2, m1, (k2 tog) twice, m2, sl 1, k1, psso, k3, m1, (k2 tog) twice, m2, sl 1, k1, psso, k2, (m1, k2 tog) 3 times, m1, k2.
Row 6: M1, k2 tog, k11, p1, k8, p1, k6.
Row 7: Sl 1, k18, (m1, k2 tog) 4 times, m1, k2 (30 sts).

Row 8: M1, k2 tog, k28.
Row 9: Sl 1, k2, m1, (k2 tog) twice, m2, sl 1, k1, psso, k3, m1, (k2 tog) twice, m2, sl 1, k1, psso, (m1, k2 tog) 5 times, m1, k2.
Row 10: M1, k2 tog, k13, p1, k8, p1, k6.
Row 11: Sl 1, k17, k2 tog, (m1, k2 tog) 5 times, k1.
Row 12: M1, k2 tog, k28.
Row 13: Sl 1, k2, m1, (k2 tog) twice, m2, sl 1, k1, psso, k3, m1, (k2 tog) twice, m2, sl 1, k1, psso, k1, k2 tog, (m1, k2 tog) 4 times, k1.
Row 14: M1, k2 tog, k11, p1, k8, p1, k6.
Row 15: Sl 1, k19, k2 tog, (m1, k2 tog) 3 times, k1.
Row 16: M1, k2 tog, k26.
Row 17: Sl 1, k2, m1, (k2 tog) twice, m2, sl 1, k1, psso, k3, m1, (k2 tog) twice, m2, sl 1, k1, psso, k3, k2 tog, (m1, k2 tog) twice, k1.
Row 18: M1, k2 tog, k9, p1, k8, p1, k6.

Row 19: Sl 1, k21, k2 tog, m1, k2 tog, k1.
Row 20: M1, k2 tog, k24.
Repeat Rows 1–20 until length desired.
Work corresponding length for other side.

Lavender bag

Repeat coathanger pattern once.
Cast off.
Make another piece, and sew the 2 pieces together.
Thread ribbon through holes. Insert lavender and decorate with tiny bow.

MAVIS

Coathanger

Cast on 18 sts. Knit one row.
Row 1: Sl 1, k3, m1, k2 tog, k4, k2 tog, m2, k2 tog, m1, k2 tog, k1, m3, k1 (21 sts).
Row 2: K2, p1, k6, p1, k11.
Row 3: Sl 1, k4, m1, k2 tog, k8, m1, k2 tog, k4.
Row 4: K21.
Row 5: Sl 1, k5, m1, k2 tog, k2, k2 tog, m2, k2 tog, k2, m1, k2 tog, k3.
Row 6: Cast off 3 sts, k5, p1, k11 (18 sts).
Row 7: Sl 1, k6, m1, k2 tog, k5, m1, k2 tog, k1, m3, k1.
Row 8: K2, p1, k18.
Row 9: Sl 1, k7, m1, (k2 tog) twice, m2, k2 tog, k1, m1, k2 tog, k4.
Row 10: K9, p1, k11.
Row 11: Sl 1, k8, m1, k2 tog, k5, m1, k2 tog, k3.
Row 12: Cast off 3 sts, k17.
Repeat Rows 1–12 until length desired.
Work corresponding length for other side.

Lavender bag

Knit the coathanger pattern twice.
Cast off.
Repeat for other side.
Sew around sides and bottom. Thread fine ribbon through holes. Wrap a small quantity of lavender in muslin and place inside lavender bag.

ECKERSLEY

Coathanger

Cast on 26 sts. Knit 1 row.
Row 1: Sl 1, k2, m1, (k2 tog) twice, m2, sl 1, k1, psso, k3, m1, (k2 tog) twice, m2, sl 1, k1, psso, k1, m1, k2 tog, k3, m2, k2 tog.
Row 2: K2, (p1, k8) twice, p1, k6.
Row 3: Sl 1, k19, m1, k2 tog, k5.
Row 4: K27.
Row 5: Sl 1, k2, m1, (k2 tog) twice, m2, sl 1, k1, psso, k3, m1, (k2 tog) twice, m2, sl 1, k1, psso, k3, m1, k2 tog, k2, m2, k2 tog.
Row 6: K2, p1, k9, p1, k8, p1, k6.
Row 7: Sl 1, k21, m1, k2 tog, k4.
Row 8: K28.
Row 9: Sl 1, k2, m1, (k2 tog) twice, m2, sl 1, k1, psso, k3, m1, (k2 tog) twice, m2, sl 1, k1, psso, k5, m1, k2 tog, k1, m2, k2 tog.
Row 10: K2, p1, k10, p1, k8, p1, k6.
Row 11: Sl 1, k23, m1, k2 tog, k3.
Row 12: Cast off 3 sts, k25 (26 sts).
Repeat Rows 1–12 until length desired.
Work corresponding length for other side.

Lavender bag

Make 2 pieces thus:
Repeat coathanger pattern rows 1–12 twice.
Cast off. Sew together. Thread fine ribbon through holes.
Insert lavender.

To assemble coathangers

Pad a small piece of wood. Insert hook in centre. Sew the 2 strips of knitting together leaving space in the centre for the hook. Place over hanger. Thread ribbon through the bottom holes, linking the cover together. Cover hook with a length of ribbon or a knitted strip. Cover base of hook with a tiny bow.

28: FLUTED COVER

The little bedcover owes its charm to the simple design. It is knitted on 1.25 mm (18) needles using 3 × 20 g balls of DMC 20 Cotton.
The bed is a reproduction, the chest of drawers a scale model by Flick Evans.

Begin at pillow end of bedcover.
Cast on 110 sts.
Row 1: Knit.
Row 2: K3, purl to last 3 sts, k3.
Repeat Rows 1–2 for 28 rows.
Reverse so that wrong side is facing.
Row 1: Knit.
Row 2: K3, p to last 3 sts, k3.
Proceed until work measures 7'' (18 cm) or length required. Cast off.

Fluted edging for pillow return

Cast on 10 sts.
Row 1: Knit.
Row 2: P5, turn, k5.
Row 3: P5, k1, m1, k2 tog, k2.
Row 4: K5, p5.
Row 5: K5, turn, p5.
Row 6: Knit.

Wider fluted edging for main part of cover

Cast on 14 sts.
Row 1: Knit.
Row 2: P9, turn, k9.
Row 3: P9, k1, m1, k2 tog, k2.
Row 4: K5, p9.
Row 5: K9, turn, p9.
Row 6: Knit.
Knit both edgings for length required.

Make up

Press lightly. Attach edgings allowing ample fullness at corners. Thread ribbon through holes. Use contrasting ribbon if preferred.

29: GUNSON THE SAILOR

Reproduction Heubach doll by Pat Blyth 18'' (46 cm).
The pattern is a facsimile of the British bluejacket uniform of the nineteenth century. The uniform is knitted in Cobra 8-ply Cotton on 3 mm (11) needles. The collar is knitted in Jaeger D.K. (8-ply) Cotton on 3 mm (11) needles. Yarn requirements: 4 × 50 g balls Cobra in white. 3 × 50 g balls Cobra in navy. 2 × 50 g balls Jaeger D.K. Cotton (8 ply). Ribbons as required.
Doll from Blyth collection.

JACKET

Back

Cast on 40 sts.
Row 1: Knit.
Row 2: (P1, m1, p2 tog) to last st, k1.
Row 3–60: St st.
Row 61: Cast off 5 sts, k to end of row.
Row 62: Cast off 5 sts, p to end of row ***.
Rows 63–80: St st.
Row 81: Cast off 10 sts, k to end of row.
Row 82: Cast off 10 sts, p to end of row.
Leave remaining 10 sts on holder.

Front

Cast on 40 sts.
Work as for back until ***.
Continue on 15 sts each side.
Row 63: K4, p8, k3.
Row 64: K12, p3.
Repeat Rows 63–64 until you have worked to row 80.
Row 81: Cast off 10 sts. Leave remainder on holder.
Transfer the 20 sts from holder for collar. Collar is reversed to right side.
Row 1: Purl 20 sts.
Row 2: K twice in each st (40 sts).
Row 3: K4, p32, k4.
Row 4: Knit.
Row 5: K4, (p5, m1) to last 4 sts, k4.
Rows 6–9: St st.
Row 10: Inc every 2nd st.
Rows 11–17: Knit.
Cast off.
Sew shoulder seams.

Sleeves

Cast on 24 sts.
Rows 1–14: K2, p2, rib.
Row 15: Inc 1, (k2, p1, m1, p1) to end of row.
Row 16: Knit.
Row 17: Purl.
Rows 18 and 19: As Rows 16 and 17.
Row 20: K1, inc 1, k1 to last 2 sts, inc 1, k1.
Row 21: P1, inc 1, p to last 2 sts, inc 1, p1.
Repeat Rows 20–21 until 36 sts remain.
Row 26: Knit.
Row 27: Cast off 5 sts, p to end of row.
Row 28: Cast off 5 sts, k to end of row.

Row 29: Purl.
Row 30: Knit.
Row 31: Purl.
Rows 32–36: Dec 1 st at each end (20 sts).
Rows 37–42: St st.
Row 43: Cast off 5 sts, p to end or row.
Row 44: Cast off 5 sts, k to end of row.
Row 45: Cast off 5 sts, p to end of row.
Row 46: Cast off.
Set in sleeve. Sew underarm and side seams.

SAILOR COLLAR

Cast on 50 sts.
Knit 6 rows.
Proceed thus:
Row 7: Knit.
Row 8: K4, purl to last 4 sts, k4.
Repeat Rows 7–8 until 30 rows have been completed.
Row 37: K12 turn.
Row 38: P8, k4.
Repeat Rows 37–38 until 25 rows for one side of collar have been worked. Cut cotton and place sts on st holder. Join thread and cast off 8 sts. Work on remaining 10 sts in st st until 28 rows are completed. Knit 6 rows. Cast off. This strip is used as a brace to keep collar in position. Cast off 8 sts k, 12 sts on needle. Work to correspond with other side.
Continue thus:
K4, p8, cast on 8 sts, p8, k4 (32 sts).
K4, p24, k4. Repeat this row 3 times.
Knit 6 rows.
Cast off.
Attach 12'' (30 cm) of dark blue ribbon to bottom of brace, so ribbon can be tied securely around waist before dressing doll in sailor jacket.

UNDERVEST

Cast on 50 sts.
Rows 1–6: Knit.
Row 7: Sl 1, k2 tog, k to last 3 sts, k2 tog, k1.
Rows 8–10: Knit (48 sts).
Row 11: Sl 1, k2 tog, k42, k2 tog, k1.
Rows 12–14: Knit (46 sts).
Row 15: Sl 1, k2 tog, k40, k2 tog, k1.
Rows 16–18: Knit (44 sts).
Row 19: (K2, p2) to end of row.
Row 20: Knit.
Repeat Rows 19–20 until 50 rows are worked.
Row 69: Moss st. (K1, p1) to end of row.
Row 70: (P1, k1) to end of row.

Repeat Rows 69–70 3 times. Cast on 5 sts at end of last row.
Row 77: Knit. Cast on 5 sts at end of row (54 sts). Knit 7 rows.

Shape shoulder:
K20, k2 tog, k2, turn.
Knit, turn.
K19, k2 tog, k2 turn.
K22, turn.
K18, k2 tog, k2, turn.
K21, turn.
K17, k2 tog, k2, turn.
K20, turn.
K16, k2 tog, k2, turn.
K19, turn.
K15, k2 tog, k2, turn.
K18.
Knit 6 rows on the 18 sts.
This is top of shoulder.

Now widen shoulder:
Row 1: K16, inc 1, k2, turn.
Row 2: K19, turn.
Row 3: K17, inc 1, k2, turn.
Row 4: K20, turn.
Row 5: K18, inc 1, k2, turn.
Row 6: K21, turn.
Row 7: K19, inc 1, k2, turn.
Row 8: K22, turn.
Row 9: K20, inc 1, k2, turn.
Row 10: K23, turn.
Row 11: K21, inc 1, k2.
Cut the yarn. Leave the 24 sts on needle. Resume where you divided the sts. Cast off 6 sts for front of vest, k to end of row. Turn the work, k 2nd shoulder as above.

When you have increased the sts to 24, cast on 6 sts for back of neck and k the 24 sts of the 1st shoulder. Work back of vest on the 54 sts.
Knit 7 rows.
Next Row: Cast off 5 sts, k to end of row.
Next Row: Cast off 5 sts, work in moss st (p1, k1) to end of row (44 sts).
Work 7 rows moss st.
Then work ribbed pattern thus:
Row 1: As Row 19.
Row 2: As Row 20.
Repeat the last 2 rows for 50 rows.
Knit 4 rows.
Next Row: K2, inc 1, k to last 2 sts, inc 1, k2.
Knit 3 rows.
Repeat the increase row and 3 k rows until you have 50 sts on needle. Knit 6 rows.

Cast off.
Press lightly. Sew up sides.

N.B.: *Omit this in bride pattern (Serena, page 46).*
With light blue yarn and set of four double-pointed needles pick up 48 sts around neck. Knit one round. Cast off loosely. This makes a neat finish to neck.

TROUSERS

Cast on 35 sts for top of trouser leg.
Rows 1–2: Knit.
Row 3: Sl 1, (m1, k2 tog) to end of row.
Rows 4 and 5: Knit.
Row 6: Purl.
Row 7: K20, turn, p20, turn, k15, turn, p15, turn, k12, turn, p12, turn, k8, turn, p8, turn, k5, turn.
Row 8: Purl.
Row 9: K2, inc 1, k to end of row.
Row 10: Purl.
Row 11: Knit.
Row 12: Purl.
Row 13: K2, inc 1, k to end of row.
Row 14: Purl.
Row 15: Knit.
Row 16: Purl.
Row 17: Repeat Rows 13–16 twice (43 sts).
Row 25: K2, k2 tog, k to end of row.
Row 26: Purl (42 sts).
Divide sts onto 3 double-pointed needles. Work with 4th needle. Knit 4 rounds.
Round 5: K1, inc 1, k to last st, m1, k1.
Knit 5 rounds.
Repeat from 5th round 3 times (50 sts).
Knit 28 rounds (adjust leg length here).
Commence bell bottom flare:
K27, inc 1, k2, inc 1, k21.
Knit 1 round.
Next Round: K27, inc 1, k4, inc 1, k21.
Knit 1 round.
Next Round: K27, inc 1, k6, inc 1, k21.
Knit 5 rounds.
Work 4 rounds k1, p1, rib.
Cast off.
Turn ribbing to inside to form hem and sl st into place.

Cast on 35 sts for top of other leg.
Proceed as follows:
Rows 1 and 2: Knit.
Row 3: Sl 1, (m1, k2 tog) to end of row.
Rows 4 and 5: Knit.
Row 6: Purl.
Row 7: Knit.

Row 8: P20, turn, k20, turn, p15, turn, k15, turn, p12, turn, k12, turn, p8, turn, k8, turn, p5, turn.
Row 9: K3, inc 1, k2.
Row 10: Purl (36 sts).
Row 11: Knit.
Row 12: Purl.
Row 13: K to last 2 sts, inc 1, k2.
Row 14: Purl.
Row 15: Knit.
Row 16: Purl.
Repeat Rows 13–16 twice (43 sts).
Row 25: K to last 4 sts, k2 tog, k2.
Row 26: Purl (42 sts).
Divide sts on to double-pointed needles. Work as for 1st leg until bell bottom flare.
Next Round: K21, inc 1, k2, inc 1, k27.
Knit 1 round.
Next Round: K21, inc 1, k4, inc 1, k27.
Knit 1 round.
Next Round: K21, inc 1, k6, inc 1, k27.
Knit 5 rounds.
Work 4 rounds k1, p1, rib.
Cast off.
Hem ribbing as for 1st leg. Join legs together at front and back. Thread elastic through holes at waist and sew ends securely. Press trousers carefully. Do not press into a crease.

SAILOR HAT

Cast on 50 sts.
Rows 1–6: K2, p1, rib.
Row 7: (K3, inc 1) to end of row.
Row 8 and alternate rows: Purl.
Row 9: (K4, inc 1) to end of row.
Row 11: (K5, inc 1) to end of row.
Row 13: (K6, inc 1) to end of row.
Row 15: Knit.
Row 16: Purl.
Row 17: Knit.
Row 18: Purl.
Row 19: (K6, k2 tog) to end of row.
Row 20 and alternate rows: Purl.
Row 21: (K5, k2 tog) to end of row.
Row 23: (K4, k2 tog) to end of row.
Row 25: (K3, k2 tog) to end of row.
Row 27: (K2, k2 tog) to end of row.
Row 29: (K1, k2 tog) to end of row.
Rows 31 and 33: (K2 tog) to end of row.
Row 34: (P2 tog) to end of row.
Row 35: K2 tog.
Cast off.
Sew seam of hat. Embroider a ship's name on a length of navy ribbon and sew ribbon around hat band. Turn ribbon ends mitrewise to hang on one side. Pin cap to doll's head.

Opposite: Gunson the Sailor, Zena (page 80) and Sugar Almonds (page 82) in a delightful wedding group.

30: ZENA

Front and back

Cast on 125 sts. Knit 4 rows.
Row 1: ** K2, * k1, m1, sl 1, k1, psso, k7, k2 tog, m1, repeat from * to last 3 sts, k3.
Row 2 and alternate rows: Purl.
Row 3: K2, * k2, m1, sl 1, k1, psso, k5, k2 tog, m1, k1, repeat from * to last 3 sts, k3.
Row 5: K2, * k1, (m1, sl 1, k1, psso) twice, k3, (k2 tog, m1) twice, repeat from * to last 3 sts, k3.
Row 7: K2, * k2, (m1, sl 1, k1, psso) twice, k1, (k2 tog, m1) twice, k1, repeat from * to last 3 sts, k3.
Row 9: K2, * k1, (m1, sl 1, k1, psso) twice, m1, sl 1, k2 tog, psso, m1, (k2 tog, m1) twice, repeat from * to last 3 sts, k3.
Row 11: As Row 7.
Row 13: K2, * k3, m1, sl 1, k1, psso, m1, sl 1, k2 tog, psso, m1, k2 tog, m1, k2, repeat from * to last 3 sts, k3.
Row 15: K2, * k4, m1, sl 1, k1, psso, k1, k2 tog, m1, k3, repeat from * to last 3 sts, k3.
Row 17: K2, * k5, m1, sl 1, k2 tog, psso, m1, k4, repeat from * to last 3 sts, k3.
Row 18: Purl **.
Work **-** 5 times.

Shape waist:
Row 1: K3, * k2 tog, k2, repeat from * to end of row (95 sts).
Row 2: Purl.
Row 3: Knit.
Row 4: Purl.
Row 5: Knit.
Row 6: Purl.
Row 7: K9, * k2 tog, repeat from * to last 11 sts, k11 (57 sts).
Row 8: Purl.
Shape armholes:
Cast off 2 sts at beginning of next 2 rows. Then dec 1 st each end of next and alternate rows until 49 sts remain. Work 1 row. Leave sts on holder.

Sleeves

Cast on 53 sts. Knit 4 rows.
Work **-** of skirt pattern once.
Continue in st st. Cast off 4 sts at beginning of next 2 rows. Dec 1 st each end of next and alternate rows until 43 remain. Work 1 row. Leave remaining sts on holder.

Yoke

Sl 24 sts of back onto a spare needle. Using a set of double-pointed needles: k2 tog, k remaining sts from back holder, then sts from 1st sleeve, sts from front holder, sts from 2nd sleeve and remaining back sts left on spare needle (183 sts).
Knit 4 rows.
Next Row: K7, * k2 tog, k6, repeat from * to end of row.
Work 6 rows st st.
Repeat **-** of skirt pattern once.
Next Row: K7, * k2 tog, k5, repeat from * to end of row.
Work 3 rows in st st.
Next Row: K7, * k2 tog, k4, repeat from * to end of row.
Work 3 rows in st st.
Next Row: K1, * k2 tog, repeat from * to end of row.
Work 3 rows in st st.
Next Row: K1, * m1, k2 tog, repeat from * to end of row.
Work 3 rows in st st.
Cast off.

Right back band

Pick up 28 sts along back opening. Purl 1 row.
Next Row: K4, (m1, k2 tog) to end of row.
Purl.
Knit 1 row. Cast off.
Work left band to match, omitting buttonholes.

Make up

Press lightly. Join seams and sew in sleeves. Sew on buttons. Use ribbons as desired.

Reproduction doll by Ria Warke 16'' (41 cm).
The beautiful lace gown by Edna Lomas is knitted on 2 mm (14) needles, with a set of
double-pointed needles for the neck. Small buttons for back of dress. Add veil and flowers. You
will require 4 × 20 g balls of DMC 20 Cotton.
Doll from author's collection.

31: SUGAR ALMONDS

Antique Heubach doll 16'' (41 cm).
This delicate pink dress, in similar style to that of the bride, was knitted on 2 mm (14)
needles using 4 × 20 g balls of DMC 20 Cotton.
Doll from author's collection.

Skirt front and back

Cast on 143 sts. Knit 4 rows, then work 24 rows in st st.
Work skirt shaping:
Row 1: * K7, k2 tog, k12, repeat from * to last 17 sts, k7, k2 tog, k8.

Work 7 rows st st.
Row 9: * K7, k2 tog, k11, repeat from * to last 16 sts, k7, k2 tog, k7.
Work 7 rows st. st.
Row 16: * K6, k2 tog, k11, repeat from * to last 15 sts, k6, k2 tog, k7.

Continue decreasing this way until you work * K1, k2 tog, k11, repeat from * to last 7 sts, k7 (87 sts).
Work 17 rows st st.
Shape waist:
(K3, k2 tog, k1) to end of row (59 sts).
Knit 3 rows.
Cast off 2 sts at beginning of next 2 rows.
Dec 1 st each end of next and alternate rows until 49 sts remain.
Knit 1 row. Leave sts on holder.

Sleeves

Cast on 53 sts. Knit 4 rows.
Row 1: K2, * k1, m1, sl 1, k1, psso, k7, k2 tog, m1, repeat from * to last 3 sts, k3.
Row 2 and alternate rows: Purl.
Row 3: K2, * k2, m1, sl 1, k1, psso, k5, k2 tog, m1, k1, repeat from * to last 3 sts, k3.
Row 5: K2, * k1, (m1, sl 1, k1, psso) twice, k3, (k2 tog, m1) twice, repeat from * to last 3 sts. k3.
Row 7: K2, * k2, (m1, sl 1, k1, psso) twice, k1, repeat from * to last 3 sts, k3.
Row 9: K2, * k1, (m1, sl 1, k1, psso) twice, m1, sl 1, k2 tog, psso, m1, (k2 tog, m1) twice, repeat from * to last 3 sts, k3.
Row 11: As Row 7.
Row 13: K2, * k3, m1, sl 1, k1, psso, m1, sl 1, k2 tog, psso, m1, k2 tog, m1, k2, repeat from * to last 3 sts, k3.
Row 15: K2, * k4, m1, sl 1, k1, psso, k1, k2 tog, m1, k3, repeat from * to last 3 sts, k3.
Row 17: K2, * k5, m1, sl 1, k2 tog, psso, m1, k4, repeat from * to last 3 sts, k3.
Row 18: Purl.
Shape top of sleeve:
Cast off 4 sts at beginning of next 2 rows, then dec at each end of next and alternate rows until 43 sts remain.
Work 1 row. Leave sts on holder.

Yoke

Sl 24 sts of back on to a spare needle. Using set of double-pointed needles: k2 tog, k remaining sts from back holder, then sts from 1st sleeve, front, 2nd sleeve and remaining back sts left on spare needle (183 sts), turn. Work on 2 needles in rows.
Knit 4 rows.

Work in yoke pattern thus:
Row 1: K7, * k2 tog, k6, repeat from * to end of row (161 sts).
Work 6 rows st st.

Continue yoke pattern thus:
Row 1: K2, * k1, m1, sl 1, k1, psso, k7, k2 tog, m1, repeat from * to last 3 sts, k3.
Row 2 and alternate rows: Purl.
Row 3: K2, * k2, m1, sl 1, k1, psso, k5, k2 tog, m1, k1, repeat from * to last 3 sts, k3.
Row 5: K2, * k1, (m1, sl 1, k1, psso) twice, k3, (k2 tog, m1) twice, repeat from * to last 3 sts, k3.
Row 7: K2, * k2, (m1, sl 1, k1, psso) twice, k1, (k2 tog, m1) twice, k1, repeat from * to last 3 sts, k3.
Row 9: K2, * k1, (m1, sl 1, k1, psso) twice, m1, sl 1, k2 tog, psso, m1, (k2 tog, m1) twice, repeat from * to last 3 sts, k3.
Row 11: As Row 7.
Row 13: K2, * k3, m1, sl 1, k1, psso, m1, sl 1, k2 tog, psso, m1, k2 tog, m1, k2, repeat from * to last 3 sts, k3.
Row 15: K2, * k4, m1, sl 1, k1, psso, k1, k2 tog, m1, k3, repeat from * to last 3 sts, k3.
Row 17: K2, * k5, m1, sl 1, k2 tog, psso, m1, k4, repeat from * to last 3 sts, k3.
Row 18: Purl.
Next Row: K7, * k2 tog, k5, repeat from * to end of row.
Work 3 rows st st.
Next Row: K7, * k2 tog, k4, repeat from * to end of row.
Work 3 rows st st.
Next Row: K1, * k2 tog, repeat from * to end of row.
Work 3 rows st st.
Next Row: K1, * m1, k2 tog, repeat from * to end of row.
Work 3 rows st st.
Cast off.

Right back band

With right side facing pick up 24 sts on right side of opening.
Purl one row.
Next Row: K2, (m1, k2 tog, k5) 3 times.
Next Row: Purl.
Repeat last 2 rows once. Cast off.

Left back band

Work as right band, omitting buttonholes.

Make up

Press lightly. Join side, armhole and sleeve seams. Sew on buttons. Thread ribbon through holes. Tie in bows. Crochet shell edging around skirt and neck thus:
(2 dc, 2 ch, 2 dc) into same st, (1 ch, 2 dc, 2 ch, 2 dc) into next st. Fasten off.

32: VICTORIA POINT LACE

A superbly knitted tablecloth by Edna Lomas with a diameter of 30'' (76 cm). It was knitted on a pair of 2 mm (14) needles using 6 × 20 g balls of DMC 20 Blanc Cotton.

N.B.: Care is needed in working the following rows. Attention to DOUBLE BRACKETS in rows 131, 133, 135, 137, 139.

The tablecloth is worked in 4 sections with two identical repeats in each section. Use a marker between the 2 repeats to facilitate checking stitch numbers.

First section

Cast on 8 sts. Work a foundation row thus:
K1, p2, k1, place marker, k1, p2, k1.
Row 1 (right side): * K2, m1, k2, repeat from * to end of row.
Row 2: * K1, p3, k1, repeat from * to end of row.

Row 3: * K2, m1, k1, m1, k2, repeat from * to end of row (14 sts).
Row 4: * K1, p5, k1, repeat from * to end of row.
Row 5: * K2, m1, k2 tog, m2, k1, m1, k2, repeat from * to end of row (20 sts).
Row 6 and alternate rows: * K1, work (p1, k1) in m2 of previous row, p to last st, k1, repeat from * to end of row.
Row 7: * K1, m1, (k2 tog, m2, sl 1, k1, psso) twice, m1, k1, repeat from * to end of row (24 sts).
Row 9: *K 2, m1, sl 1, k1, psso, k2 tog, m2, sl 1, k1, psso, k2 tog, m1, k2, repeat from * to end of row.
Row 11: * K1, m1, k1, (k2 tog, m2, sl 1, k1, psso) twice, k1, m1, k1, repeat from * to end of row (28 sts).
Row 13: * K1, m1, (k2 tog, m2, sl 1, k1, psso) 3 times, m1, k1, repeat from * to end of row (32 sts).
Row 15: * K2, m1, sl 1, k1, psso, (k2 tog, m2, sl 1, k1,

psso) twice, k2 tog, m1, k2, repeat from * to end of row (34 sts).

Row 17: * K1, m1, k1, (k2 tog, m2, sl 1, k1, psso) 3 times, k1, m1, k1, repeat from * to end of row (36 sts).

Row 19: * K1, m1, (k2 tog, m2, sl 1, k1, psso) 4 times, m1, k1, repeat from * to end of row (40 sts).

Row 21: * K2, m1, sl 1, k1, psso, (k2 tog, m2, sl 1, k1, psso) 3 times, k2 tog, m1, k2, repeat from * to end of row (42 sts).

Row 23: * K1, m1, k1, (k2 tog, m2, sl 1, k1, psso) 4 times, k1, m1, k1, repeat from * to end of row (44 sts).

Row 25: * K1, m1, (k2 tog, m2, sl 1, k1, psso) 5 times, m1, k1, repeat from * to end of row (48 sts).

Row 27: * K2, m1, sl 1, k1, psso, (k2 tog, m2, sl 1, k1, psso) 4 times, k2 tog, m1, k2, repeat from * to end of row (50 sts).

Row 29: * K1, m1, k1, (k2 tog, m2, sl 1, k1, psso) 5 times, k1, m1, k1, repeat from * to end of row (50 sts).

Row 31: * K1, m1, (k2 tog, m2, sl 1, k1, psso) 6 times, m1, k1, repeat from * to end of row (56 sts).

Row 33: * K2, m1, sl 1, k1, psso, (k2 tog, m2, sl 1, k1, psso) 5 times, k2, tog, m1, k2, repeat from * to end of row (58 sts).

Row 35: * K1, m1, k1, (k2 tog, m2, sl 1, k1, psso) 6 times, k1, m1, k1, repeat from * to end of row (60 sts).

Row 37: * K1, m1, (k2 tog, m2, sl 1, k1, psso) 7 times, m1, k1, repeat from * to end of row (64 sts).

Row 39: * K2, m1, sl 1, k1, psso, (k2 tog, m2, sl 1, k1, psso) 6 times, k2 tog, m1, k2, repeat from * to end of row.

Row 41: * K1, m1, k1, (k2 tog, m2, sl 1, k1, psso) 7 times, k1, m1, k1, repeat from * to end of row (68 sts).

Row 43: * K1, m1, (k2 tog, m2, sl 1, k1, psso) 8 times, m1, k1, repeat from * to end of row (72 sts).

Row 45: * K1, k1 tbl, m1, sl 1, k1, psso, (k2 tog, m2, sl 1, k1, psso) 7 times, k2 tog, m1, k1 tbl, k1, repeat from * to end of row.

Row 47: * K1, m1, k1 tbl, m1, (k2 tog, m2, sl 1, k1, psso) 8 times, m1, k1 tbl, m1, k1, repeat from * to end of row (80 sts).

Row 49: * K1, (m1, k1 tbl) 3 times, m1, sl 1, k1, psso, (k2 tog, m2, sl 1, k1, psso) 7 times, k2 tog, (m1, k1 tbl) 3 times, m1, k1, repeat from * to end of row (92 sts).

Row 51: * K2 tog, (m1, k1 tbl) 5 times, (k2 tog, m2, sl 1, k1, psso) 8 times, (k1 tbl, m1) 5 times, k2 tog, repeat from * to end of row (108 sts).

Row 53: * K2 tog, m1, sl 1, k1, psso, (k1, m1) twice, k1 tbl, (m1, k1) twice, k2 tog, m1, sl 1, k1, psso, (k2 tog, m2, sl 1, k1, psso) 7 times, k2 tog, m1, sl 1, k1, psso, (k1, m1) twice, k1 tbl, (m1, k1) twice, k2 tog, m1, sl 1, k1, psso, repeat from * to end of row (116 sts).

Row 55: * K2 tog, m1, sl 1, k1, psso, k2, m1, k1, m1, k1 tbl, m1, k1, m1, k2, k2 tog, (k2 tog, m2, sl 1, k1, psso) 8 times, sl 1, k1, psso,k2, m1, k1, m1, k1 tbl, m1, k1, m1, k2, k2 tog, m1, sl 1, k1, psso, repeat from * to end of row (124 sts).

Row 57: * K2 tog, m1, sl 1, k1, psso, k3, m1, k1, m1, k1 tbl, m1, k1, m1, k3, k2 tog, sl 1, k1, psso, (k2 tog, m2, sl 1, k1, psso) 7 times, k2 tog, sl 1, k1, psso, k3, m1, k1, m1, k1 tbl, m1, k1, m1, k3, k2 tog, m1, sl 1, k1, psso, repeat from * to end of row (128 sts).

Row 59: * K2 tog, m1, sl 1, k1, psso, k5, m1, k1 tbl, m1, k5, k2 tog, m1, sl 1, k2 tog, psso, (k2 tog, m2, sl 1, k1, psso) 6 times, k3 tog, m1, sl 1, k1, psso, k5, m1, k1 tbl, m1, k5, k2 tog, m1, sl 1, k1, psso, repeat from * to end of row (124 sts).

Row 61: * (K1, m1) twice, sl 1, k1, psso, k11, k2 tog, m1, k1 tbl, m1, sl 1, k2 tog, psso, (k2 tog, m2, sl 1, k1, psso) 5 times, k3 tog, m1, k1 tbl, m1, sl 1, k1, psso, k11, k2 tog, (m1, k1) twice, repeat from * to end of row.

Row 63: * K1, m1, k1, m2, sl 1, k1, psso, m1, sl 1, k1, psso, k9, k2 tog, (m1, k1 tbl) 3 times, m1, sl 1, k2 tog, psso, (k2 tog, m2, sl 1, k1, psso) 4 times, k3 tog, (m1, k1 tbl) 3 times, m1 sl 1, k1, psso, k9, k2 tog, m1, k2 tog, m2, k1, m1, k1, repeat from * to end of row (136 sts).

Row 65: * (k1, m1) twice, sl 1, k1, psso, k2 tog, m2, k1, m1, sl 1, k1, psso, k7, k2 tog, sl 1, k1, psso, (m1, k1 tbl) 3 times, m1, k2 tog, sl 1, k2 tog, psso, (k2 tog, m1, sl 1, k1, psso) 3 times, k3 tog, sl 1, k1, psso, (m1, k1 tbl) 3 times, m1, k2 tog, sl 1, k1, psso, k7, k2 tog, m1, k1, m2, sl 1, k1, psso, k2 tog, (m1, k1) twice, repeat from * to end of row (140 sts).

Row 67: * K1, m1, sl 1, k1, psso, k2 tog, m2, sl 1, k1, psso, k2 tog, m1, k1, m1, sl 1, k1, psso, k5, k2 tog, sl 1, k1, psso, (k1, m1) twice, k1 tbl, (m1, k1) twice, k2 tog, sl 1, k2 tog, psso, (k2 tog, m2, sl 1, k1, psso) twice, k3 tog, sl 1, k1, psso, (k1, m1) twice, k1 tbl, (m1, k1) twice, k2 tog, sl 1, k1, psso, k5, k2 tog, m1, k1, m1, sl 1, k1, psso, k2 tog, m2, sl 1, k1, psso, k2 tog, m1, k1, repeat from * to end of row (136 sts).

Row 69: * K1, (k2 tog, m2, sl 1, k1, psso) twice, (k1, m1) twice, sl 1, k1, psso, k3, k2 tog, sl 1, k1, psso, k2, m1, k1, m1, k1 tbl, m1, k1, m1, k2, k2 tog, sl 1, k2 tog, psso, k2 tog, m2, sl 1, k1, psso, k3 tog, sl 1, k1, psso, k2, m1, k1, m1, k1 tbl, m1, k1, m1, k2, k2 tog, sl 1, k1, psso, k3, k2 tog, (m1, k1) twice, (k2 tog, m2, sl 1, k1, psso) twice, k1, repeat from * to end of row.

Row 71: * K1, m1, sl 1, k1, psso, (k2 tog, m2, sl 1, k1 psso) twice, (k1, m1) twice, sl 1, k1, psso, k1, k2 tog, sl 1, k1, psso, k3, m1, k1, m1, k1 tbl, m1, k1, m1, k3, k2 tog, sl 1, k2 tog, psso, k3 tog, sl 1, k1, psso, k3, m1, k1, m1, k1 tbl, m1, k1, m1, k3, k2 tog, sl 1, k1, psso, k1, k2 tog, (m1, k1) twice, (k2 tog, m2, sl 1, k1, psso) twice, k2 tog, m1, k1, repeat from * to end of row.

Row 73: * K1, (k2 tog, m2, sl 1, k1, psso) 3 times, k2 tog, m2, sl 1, k2 tog, psso, sl 1, k1, psso, k5, m1, k1 tbl, m1, k5, (k2 tog) twice, sl 1, k1, psso, k5, m1, k1 tbl, m1, k5, k2 tog, sl 1, k2 tog, psso, m2, sl 1, k1, psso, (k2 tog, m2, sl 1, k1, psso) 3 times, k1, repeat from * to end of row (130 sts).

Row 75: * K1, m1, sl 1, k1, psso, (k2 tog, m2, sl 1, k1,

psso) 3 times, k2 tog, m1, sl 1, k1, psso, k11, k2 tog, m1, k1 tbl, m1, sl 1, k1, psso, k11, k2 tog, m1, sl 1, k1, psso, (k2 tog, m2, sl 1, k1, psso) 3 times, k2 tog, m1, k1, repeat from * to end of row (126 sts).

Row 77: * K1, (k2 tog, m2, sl 1, k1, psso) 4 times, m1, sl 1, k1, psso, k9, k2 tog, (m1, k1 tbl) 3 times, m1, sl 1, k1, psso, k9, k2 tog, m1, (k2 tog, m2, sl 1, k1, psso) 4 times, k1, repeat from * to end of row (130 sts).

Row 79: * K1, m1, sl 1, k1, psso, (k2 tog, m2, sl 1, k1, psso) 3 times, k2 tog, m1, k1, m1, sl 1, k1, psso, k7, k2 tog, sl 1, k1, psso, (m1, k1 tbl) 3 times, m1, k2 tog, sl 1, k1, psso, k7, k2 tog, m1, k1, m1, sl 1, k1, psso, (k2 tog, m2, sl 1, k1, psso) 3 times, k2 tog, m1, k1, repeat from * to end of row.

Row 81: * K1, (k2 tog, m2, sl 1, k1, psso) 4 times, (k1, m1) twice, sl 1, k1, psso, k5, k2 tog, sl 1, k1, psso, (k1, m1) twice, k1 tbl, (m1, k1) twice, k2 tog, sl 1, k1, psso, k5, k2 tog, (m1, k1) twice, (k2 tog, m2, sl 1, k1, psso) 4 times, k1, repeat from * to end of row (135 sts).

Row 83: * K1, m1, sl 1, k1, psso, (k2 tog, m2, sl 1, k1, psso) 4 times, (k1, m1) twice, sl 1, k1, psso, k3, k2 tog, sl 1, k1, psso, k2, m1, k1, m1, k1 tbl, m1, k1, m1, k2, k2 tog, sl 1, k1, psso, k3, k2 tog, (m1, k1) twice, (k2 tog, m2, sl 1, k1, psso) 4 times, k2 tog, m1, k1, repeat from * to end of row (138 sts).

Row 85: * K1, (k2 tog, m2, sl 1, k1, psso) 5 times, (k1, m1) twice, sl 1, k1, psso, k1, k2 tog, sl 1, k1, psso, k3, m1, k1, m1, k1 tbl, m1, k1, m1, k3, k2 tog, sl 1, k1, psso, k1, k2 tog, (m1, k1) twice, (k2 tog, m2, sl 1, k1, psso) 5 times, k1, repeat from * to end of row (142 sts).

Row 87: * K1, m1, sl 1, k1, psso, (k2 tog, m2, sl 1, k1, psso) 5 times, k2 tog, m2, sl 1, k2 tog, psso, sl 1, k1, psso, k5, m1, k1 tbl, m1, k5, k2 tog, sl 1, k2 tog, psso, (m2, sl 1, k1, psso, k2 tog) 6 times, m1, k1, repeat from * to end of row (138 st).

Row 89: * K1, (k2 tog, m2, sl 1, k1, psso) 6 times, k2 tog, m1, sl 1, k1, psso, k11, k2 tog, m1, (sl 1, k1, psso, k2 tog, m2) 6 times, sl 1, k1, psso, k1, repeat from * to end of row (134 sts).

Row 91: * K1, m1, (sl 1, k1, psso, k2 tog, m2) 6 times, sl 1, k1, psso, m1, sl 1, k1, psso, k9, k2 tog, m1, (k2 tog, m2, sl 1, k1, psso) 6 times, k2 tog, m1, k1, repeat from * to end of row.

Row 93: * K1, m1, (k2 tog, m2, sl 1, k1, psso) 6 times, k2 tog, m1, k1, m1, sl 1, k1, psso, k7, k2 tog, m1, k1, m1, (sl 1, k1, psso, k2 tog, m2) 6 times, sl 1, k1, psso, m1, k1, repeat from * to end of row (138 sts).

Row 95: * (K1, m1) twice, (sl 1, k1, psso, k2 tog, m2) 6 times, sl 1, k1, psso, (k1, m1) twice, sl 1, k1, psso, k5, k2 tog, (m1, k1) twice, (k2 tog, m2, sl 1, k1, psso) 6 times, k2 tog, (m1, k1) twice, repeat from * to end of row (146 sts).

Row 97: * (K2, m1) twice, k1, (m2, sl 1, k1, psso, k2 tog) 6 times, m2, sl 1, k1, psso, (k1, m1) twice, sl 1, k1, psso, k3, k2 tog, (m1, k1) twice, (k2 tog, m2, sl 1, k1,

psso) 6 times, k2 tog, m2, k1, (m1, k2) twice, repeat from * to end of row (162 sts).

Row 99: * (K3, m1) twice, (sl 1, k1, psso, k2 tog, m2) 7 times, sl 1, k1, psso, k2 tog, m1, sl 1, k1, psso, k1, k2 tog, m1, (sl 1, k1, psso, k2 tog, m2) 7 times, sl 1, k1, psso, k2 tog, (m1, k3) twice, repeat from * to end of row.

Row 101: * (K4, m1) twice, k1, (m2, sl 1, k1, psso, k2 tog) 7 times, m2, sl 1, k1, psso, sl 1, k2, tog, psso, (k2 tog, m2, sl 1, k1, psso) 7 times, k2 tog, m2, k1, (m1, k4) twice, repeat from * to end of row (170 sts).

Row 103: * (k5, m1) twice, (sl 1, k1, psso, k2 tog, m2) 8 times, k into f and b of next st, (m2, sl 1, k1, psso, k2 tog) 8 times, (m1, k5) twice, repeat from * to end of row (180 sts).

Row 105: * K1, m1, sl 1, k1, psso, k3, m1, k6, m1, sl 1, k2 tog, psso, (k2 tog, m2, sl 1, k1, psso) 15 times, k3 tog, m1, k6, m1, k3, k2 tog, m1, k1, repeat from * to end of row.

Row 107: * K2, m1, sl 1, k1, psso, k3, m1, k7, m1, sl 1, k2 tog, psso, (k2 tog, m2, sl 1, k1, psso) 14 times, k3 tog, m1, k7, m1, k3, k2 tog, m1, k2, repeat from * to end of row.

Row 109: * K3, m1, k5, m1, k8, m1, sl 1, k2 tog, psso, (k2 tog, m2, sl 1, k1, psso) 13 times, k3 tog, m1, k8, m1, k5, m1, k3, repeat from * to end of row (184 sts).

Row 111: * K2, k2 tog, m1, k6, m1, k9, m1, sl 1, k2 tog, psso, (k2 tog, m2, sl 1, k1, psso) 12 times, k3 tog, m1, k9, m1, k6, m1, sl 1, k1, psso, k2, repeat from * to end of row.

Row 113: * K1, k2 tog, m1, k2, k2 tog, m1, k4, m1, k10, m1, sl 1, k2 tog, psso, (k2 tog, m2, sl 1, k1, psso) 11 times, k3 tog, m1, k10, m1, k4, m1, sl 1, k1, psso, k2, m1, sl 1, k1, psso, k1, repeat from * to end of row.

Row 115: * K2 tog, m1, k2, k2 tog, m1, k6, m1, sl 1, k1, psso, k7, k2 tog, m1, sl 1, k2 tog, psso, (k2 tog, m2, sl 1, k1, psso) 10 times, k3 tog, m1, sl 1, k1, psso, k7, k2 tog, m1, k6, m1, sl 1, k1, psso, k2, m1, sl 1, k1, psso, repeat from * to end of row (176 sts).

Row 117: * K3, (k2 tog, m1) twice, k1, m1, sl 1, k1, psso, k3, m1, sl 1, k1, psso, k6, k2 tog, m1, sl 1, k1, psso, k1, (k2 tog, m2, sl 1, k1, psso) 9 times, k1, k2 tog, m1, sl 1, k1, psso, k6, k2 tog, m1, k3, k2 tog, m1, k1, (m1, sl 1, k1, psso) twice, k3, repeat from * to end of row (172 sts).

Row 119: * K2, (k2 tog, m1) twice, k3, m1, k5, m1, sl 1, k1, psso, k5, k2 tog, m1, sl 1, k1, psso, (m2, sl 1, k1, psso, k2 tog) 9 times, m2, k2 tog, m1, sl 1, k1, psso, k5, k2 tog, m1, k5, m1, k3, (m1, sl 1, k1, psso) twice, k2, repeat from * to end of row (176 sts).

Row 121: * K1, (k2 tog, m1) twice, k5, m1, k6, m1, sl 1, k1, psso, k4, k2 tog, m1, (sl 1, k1, psso, k2 tog, m2) 9 times, sl 1, k1, psso, k2 tog, m1, sl 1, k1, psso, k4, k2 tog, m1, k6, m1, k5, (m1, sl 1, k1, psso) twice, k1, repeat from * to end of row.

Row 123: * (K2 tog, m1) twice, k2, k2 tog, k3, m1, k7, m1, sl 1, k1, psso, k3, k2 tog, m1, k1, m1, (sl 1, k1, psso, k2 tog, m2) 8 times, sl 1, k1, psso, k2 tog, m1, k1, m1, sl 1, k1, psso, k3, k2 tog, m1, k7, m1, k3, sl 1, k1, psso, k2, (m1, sl 1, k1, psso) twice, repeat from * to end of row.

Row 125: * K1, k2 tog, m1, k2, k2 tog, m2, sl 1, k1, psso, k8, k2 tog, m2, sl 1, k1, psso, k2, k2 tog, m1, k1, (k2 tog, m2, sl 1, k1, psso) 9 times, k1, m1, sl 1, k1, psso, k2, k2 tog, m2, sl 1, k1, psso, k8, k2 tog, m2, sl 1, k1, psso, k2, m1, sl 1, k1, psso, k1, repeat from * to end of row.

Row 127: * K2 tog, m1, k2, k2 tog, m1, k2 tbl, m1, sl 1, k1, psso, k6, k2 tog, m1, k2 tbl, m1, sl 1, k1, psso, k1, k2 tog, m1, k1, sl 1, k1, psso, k1, k2 tog, (m1, k2 tbl, m1, sl 1, k1, psso, k1, k2 tog, m2, sl 1, k1, psso, k1, k2 tog) twice, m1, k2 tbl, m1, sl 1, k1, psso, k1, k2 tog, k1, m1, sl 1, k1, psso, k1, k2 tog, m1, k2 tbl, m1, sl 1, k1, psso, k6, k2 tog, m1, k2 tbl, m1, sl 1, k1, psso, k2, m1, sl 1, k1, psso, repeat from * to end of row (172 sts).

Row 129: * K3, k2 tog, m1, k2 tog, m2, sl 1, k1, psso, m1, sl 1, k1, psso, k4, k2 tog, m1, k2 tog, m2, sl 1, k1, psso, m1, sl 1, k1, psso, k2 tog, m1, (k2, k2 tog, m1, k2 tog, m2, sl 1, k1, psso, m1, sl 1, k1, psso, k2) 3 times, m1, sl 1, k1, psso, k2 tog, m1, k2 tog, m2, sl 1, k1, psso, m1, sl 1, k1, psso, k4, k2 tog, m1, k2 tog, m2, sl 1, k1, psso, m1, sl 1, k1, psso, k3, repeat from * to end of row.

Row 131 (note double brackets in this row): * K2, (k2 tog, m1) twice, k2 tbl, (m1, sl 1, k1, psso) twice, k2, (k2 tog, m1) twice, k2 tbl, m1, sl 1, k1, psso, m1, sl 1, k2 tog, psso, m1 [(k1, (k2 tog, m1) twice, k2 tbl, (m1, sl 1, k1, psso) twice, k1)] 3 times, m1 sl 1, k2 tog, psso, m1, k2 tog, m1, k2 tbl, (m1, sl 1, k1, psso) twice, k2, (k2 tog, m1) twice, k2 tbl, (m1, sl 1, k1, psso) twice, k2, repeat from * to end of row.

Row 133 (note double brackets in this row): * K1, [(k2 tog, (m1, k2 tog) twice, m2, (sl 1, k1, psso, m1) twice, sl 1, k1, psso)] 7 times, k1, repeat from * to end of row.

Row 135 (note double brackets in this row): * K2 tog, [(m1, (k2 tog, m1) twice, k2 tbl, (m1, sl 1, k1, psso) 3 times)] 4 times, [(m1, (k2 tog, m1) twice, k2 tbl, m1, (sl 1, k1, psso, m1) twice, k2 tog)] 3 times, repeat from * to end of row (184 sts).

Row 137 (note double brackets in this row): * [(K1 tbl (m1, k2 tog) twice, m1, k4, (m1, sl 1, k1, psso) twice, m1)] 7 times, k1 tbl, repeat from * to end of row (212 sts).

Row 139 (note double brackets in this row): * [(K1 tbl, (m1, k2 tog) twice, m1, k6, (m1, sl 1, k1, psso) twice, m1)] 7 times, k1 tbl, repeat from * to end of row (240 sts).

Row 140: * K1, p to last st before marker, k1, repeat from * to end of row (240 sts).

Cut thread leaving a length of approximately 26'' (66 cm)). Leave work on a spare needle.

Knit 3 more sections. Do not cut thread after knitting 4th section.

Crochet edging

With right side of 4th section facing knit 2 sts and slip on to a safety pin. Insert crochet hook into next 3 sts and draw through thread. * (10 ch, 1 dc, into next 4 sts) twice, (10 ch, 1 dc into next 3 sts) 3 times. Repeat from * to last 13 sts of section, (10 ch, 1 dc into next 4 sts) twice, 10 ch, 1 dc into next 3 sts. ** Sl last 2 sts on to needle with next section. 10 ch, 1 dc into next 4 sts, 10 ch, 1 dc into next 3 sts. ***

Repeat from *–*** twice and from * to ** once. Sl 2 sts from safety pin on to end of needle, 10 dc into next 4 sts, 10 ch, 1 sl st into 1 st, st. Cut thread, leaving a length of approximately 26'' (66 cm). Secure the join of the crochet edging, then work thread back through the last 2 sts.

Make up

Using a flat seam, join garter st edgings of 2 sections starting at outer edge of cloth, and working towards centre. When 2 adjoining cast on sts have been sewn together stretch the seam carefully, then sew through the last 2 sts again. Finish off the seam by threading yarn through the seam on wrong side.

Neaten centre:

With 1 length of thread left at beginning of cast on row, pick up 1 loop of each of the 32 sts. Pull sts together and fasten thread on wrong side. Complete the other 3 sections. Press lightly. Pin out loops if desired.

33: MERRY MAIDEN

Reproduction doll by Pat Blyth 18'' (46 cm).
A delicate floor-length gown knitted on 2.75 mm (12) needles with 6 × 20 g balls of DMC
20 Blanc Cotton. The bodice and sleeves are worked on 2.25 mm (13) needles. The collar is
knitted on 1 mm (20) needles using DMC 100 Cotton in the Dunbar Rose Lace pattern. Four
small buttons are required.
Doll from Blyth collection.

Back

Cast on 154 sts. Knit 2 rows.
Row 3: Sl 1, * k1, m1, k2, sl 1, k2 tog, psso, k2, m1, repeat from * to last st, k1.
Row 4: Sl 1, purl to last st. k1.
Row 5: Sl 1, * k2, m1, k1, sl 1, k2 tog, psso, k1, m1, k1, repeat from * to last st, k1.
Row 6: Sl 1, purl to last st, k1.
Row 7: Sl 1, * k3, m1, sl 1, k2, tog, psso, m1, k2, repeat from * to last st, k1.
Row 8: Sl 1, purl to last st, k1.
Repeat Rows 3–8 until 11 patterns have been worked (adjust length here). Then work Rows 3–7 once.
Next Row: K2 tog, (p2 tog) 30 times, (p3 tog) 10 times, (p2 tog) 30 times, k2 tog (72 sts).
Next Row: * K2 tog, m1, k2, repeat from * to end of row.
Next Row: Sl 1, purl to last 2 sts, inc 1 in next st purlwise, k1 (73 sts).
Proceed as follows:
Row 1: Sl 1, k1, * p1, k1, repeat from * to last st, k1.
Repeat Row 1 9 times * *.
Divide for back opening:
Next Row: Sl 1, (k1, p1) 19 times, turn (39 sts on needle).
Row 1: Sl 1, k1, * p1, k1, repeat from * to last st, k1, repeat row 1 4 times.

Armhole

Row 1: Cast off 4 sts, work in pattern to last st, k1.
Row 2: Sl 1, work in pattern to last st, k1.
Row 3: K2 tog, work in pattern to last 3 sts, m1, k2 tog, k1.
Row 4: Sl 1, k1, * p1, k1, repeat from * to end of row.
Work 32 rows in pattern, decreasing once at armhole in next and every alternate row; at the same time work a buttonhole in 17th row (18 sts).
Break off yarn. Leave sts on holder.
Next Row: Cast on 5 sts using same needle with right side facing. Work in pattern across the remaining 34 sts, thus. (P1, k1) 17 times (39 sts).
Proceed as follows on these 39 sts:
Row 1: Sl 1, k1, * p1, k1, repeat from * to last st, k1.
Repeat Row 1 5 times.
Armhole shaping:
Row 1: Cast off 4 sts, work in pattern to last st, k1. Work 34 rows, decreasing once at armhole edge in next and every alternate row (18 sts). Do not break yarn. Leave sts on holder.

Front

Cast on 154 sts. Knit 2 rows. Work as for back of dress until **.
Work 6 rows in pattern.
Shape armholes:
Cast off 4 sts at beginning of next 2 rows. Work 20 rows in pattern, decreasing once at each end of the next and every alternate row (45 sts).

Shape neck:
Next Row: K2 tog, pattern 14 sts, turn.
Proceed as follows on these 15 sts.
Next Row: Sl 1, pattern 13 sts, k1.
Work 7 rows in pattern, decreasing once at armhole edge in next and every alternate row, at the same time decreasing once at neck edge in every row (4 sts).
Next Row: Sl 1, pattern 2 sts, k1.
Next Row: K2 tog, pattern 1 st, k1.
Next Row: Sl 1, pattern 1 st, k1.
Next Row: K2 tog, k1.
Next Row: K2 tog.
Break off yarn. Fasten off.
With right side facing, sl 13 sts onto a thread. Rejoin yarn and proceed as follows on remaining 16 sts:
Next Row: K1, work in pattern to last 2 sts, k2 tog.
Next Row: Sl 1, work in pattern to last st, k1.
Work 7 rows, decreasing once at neck edge in every row, at the same time decreasing once at armhole edge in next and every alternate row (4 sts).
Next Row: Sl 1, pattern 2 sts, k1.
Next Row: Sl 1, pattern 1 st, k2 tog.
Next Row: Sl 1, pattern 1 st, k1.
Next Row: Sl 1, k2 tog.
Next Row: K2 tog.
Break off yarn. Fasten off.

Sleeves

Using 2.25 mm (13) needles, cast on 42 sts and knit 4 rows.
Next Row: Work a row of holes (k2, m1, k2 tog) to end of row.
Work 2 patterns of dress skirt, then inc each end of the needle every 3rd row until 54 sts on needle. Continue in pattern until sleeve is length required. Dec every row until 11 sts remain. Leave sts on needle.

Make up

Press work lightly. Sew side and sleeve seams. Sew back underlay in position.

Neckband

With right side facing, begin at left half of neck. Work k18, knit 11 sts on sleeve. Pick up and knit 12 sts on left side of front. Work 13 sts at front of neck. Pick up and knit 12 sts on right side of front of neck. Work 11 sts on sleeve. Work 18 sts at back of neck (95 sts).

Row 1: Sl 1, k13, (k2 tog, k11) 5 times, k2 tog, k14 (89 sts).
Row 2: Sl 1, k to last 3 sts, m1, k2 tog, k1.
Row 3: Sl 1, knit to end of row.
Row 4: As Row 3.
Cast off.

Thread ribbons or fine cord through holes at waist and wrists.

Collar

DUNBAR ROSE LACE

Cast on 19 sts.
Row 1: Sl 1, k3, (m1, k2 tog, k1) twice, k2 tog, m1, k1, m1, k2 tog, k1, k2 tog, m1, (k1, p1) in last st.
Row 2: (K3, m1, sl 1, k2 tog, psso, m1) twice, k4, m1, k2 tog, k2.
Row 3: Sl 1, k3, (m1, k2 tog, k1, k2 tog, m1, k1) twice, m1, k3, (k1, p1) in last st.
Row 4: Cast off 4 sts, m1, k3, m1, sl 1, k2, tog, psso, m1, k3, (m1, k2 tog, k2) twice.
Repeat Rows 1–4 until length desired.

34: ERICA

Antique B.S.W. doll 19'' (48 cm).
Doll is wearing a lace tunic over a fluted underslip. The outfit was knitted on 2.25 mm (13) needles using 6 × 20 g balls DMC Blanc 20 Cotton. 8 small buttons for back of tunic. Doll from author's collection.

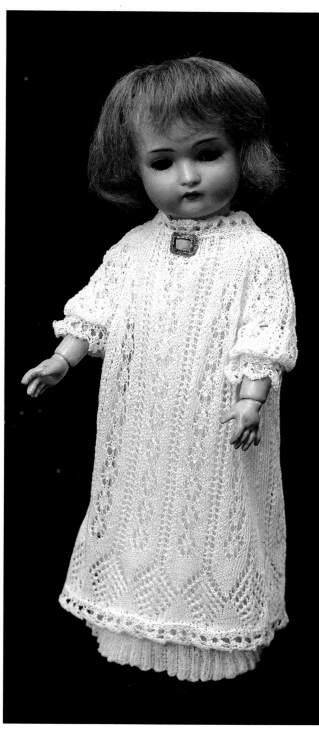

TUNIC

Back

Cast on 85 sts.
Row 1: Knit.
Row 2 and alternate rows: K1, p to last st, k1.
Row 3: * K6, m1, sl 1, k2 tog, psso, m1, k5, repeat from * to last st, k1.
Row 5: * K5, m1, k2 tog tbl, k1, k2 tog, m1, k4, repeat from * to last st, k1.
Row 7: * K4, m1, k2 tog tbl, m1, sl 1, k2 tog, psso, m1, k2 tog, m1, k3, repeat from * to last st, k1.
Row 9: * K3, (m1, k2 tog tbl) twice, k1, (k2 tog, m1) twice, k2, repeat from * to last st, k1.
Row 11: * K2, (m1, k2 tog tbl) twice, m1, sl 1, k2 tog, psso, m1, (k2 tog, m1) twice, k1, repeat from * to last st, k1.
Row 13: * K1, (m1, k2 tog tbl) 3 times, k1, (k2 tog, m1) 3 times, repeat from * to last st, k1.
Row 15: As Row 11.
Row 17: As Row 9.
Row 19: As Row 7.
Row 21: As Row 5.
Row 23: As Row 3.
Row 25: * K5, k2 tog, m1, k1, m1, k2 tog tbl, k4, repeat from * to last st, k1.
Row 27: As Row 25.
Row 29: K5, * k2 tog, m1, k1, m1, k2 tog tbl, k2, k2 tog, m1, k1, m1, k2 tog tbl, k2, repeat from * to last 10 sts, k2 tog, m1, k1, m1, k2 tog tbl, k5.
Row 31: K5, * k2 tog, m1, k1, m1, k2 tog tbl, k1, k2 tog, m1, k3, m1, k2 tog tbl, k1, repeat from * to last 10 sts, k2 tog, m1, k1, m1, k2 tog tbl, k5.
Row 33: K5, * k2 tog, m1, k1, m1, k2 tog tbl, k2, m1, k2 tog tbl, k1, k2 tog, m1, k2, repeat from * to last 10 sts, k2 tog, m1, k1, m1, k2 tog tbl, k5.
Row 35: K5, * k2 tog, m1, k1, m1, k2 tog tbl, k3, m1, sl 1, k2 tog, psso, m1, k3, repeat from * to last 10 sts, k2 tog, m1, k1, m1, k2 tog tbl, k5.
Row 36: K1, p to last st, k1.
Rows 27–36 form pattern. Continue in pattern until back measures 9'' (23 cm), ending with a wrong side row.
Keeping continuity of pattern, shape raglan as follows:
Rows 1 and 2: Cast off 5 sts, work to end of row.

Row 3: K2, k2 tog tbl, pattern to last 4 sts, k2 tog, k2.
Row 4: K1, purl to last st, k1.
Repeat Rows 3–4 until 27 sts remain ending with Row 4.
Cast off.

Right front

Cast on 43 sts. Knit 1 row.
Work in patterns Rows 1–36 as for back. Then repeat Rows 27–36 until front measures same as back to raglan shaping, ending with a wrong side row. Keeping continuity of pattern shape raglan as for back. Keeping front edge straight, work thus until 18 sts remain. Cast off.

Left front

Work to correspond with right front reversing raglan shaping.

Sleeves

Cast on 43 sts.
Work 1st 11 rows of back pattern increasing every 2nd row keeping the extra sts plain. Inc until 55 sts remain. Cast off 3 sts at each end. Knit raglans as for back until 9 sts remain.

Bands

With right side facing work left band:
Pick up and knit 80 sts along side. Knit 6 rows. Work right band the same, making 8 buttonholes evenly along front.
Cast off.

Make up

Sew up raglans and side seams.
Trim hems, cuffs and neck with the following lace:
Cast on 5 sts.
Row 1: Sl 1, k1, m2, k2 tog, k1.
Row 2: Sl 1, k2, p1, k2.
Row 3: Sl 1, k3, m2, k2.
Row 4: Sl 1, k2, p1, k4.
Row 5: Sl 1, k1, m2, k2 tog, k4.
Row 6: Sl 1, k5, p1, k2.
Row 7: Sl 1, k8.
Row 8: Cast off 4, k4.

FLUTED UNDERSLIP

The gown is worn over a simple fluted slip. The gown buttons down the back. The opening can be at the front if desired.
Cast on 150 sts.
Work in k3, p3, rib for 4½'' (11.5 cm).
Next Row: (K2 tog) to end of row (75 sts).
Work in st st for 4'' (10 cm).
Work in k1, p1, rib for 1'' (2.5 cm).
Make a row of ribbon holes in waist ribbing.
Length of underslip can be adjusted to suit your requirement.
Work other side to match.
Sew up side seams. Thread ribbon or elastic through holes. Fasten at waist.

35: BRACKEN

A modern vinyl doll 32'' (81 cm).
Doll is wearing a sports jumper in a mock cable stitch. You will require 4 × 50 g balls of 4-ply cotton. Needles: 2.75 mm (12), 3.75 mm (10) and a set of 2.75 mm (12) double-pointed needles.

Back

Using 2.75 mm (12) needles, cast on 74 sts.
Work 10 rows in k1, p1, rib.
Change to 3.25 mm (10) needles.
Row 1: (P3, k4) to end of row (dec 1 st in the row).
Row 2: (K3, p4) to end of row.
Row 3: P3, (sl 2, k2, psso) (referred to as cable 4), (p3, cable 4) to end of row.
Row 4: K3, (k twice into next 2 sts, k3) to end of row.
Row 5: (P3, k4) to end of row.
Row 6: (K3, p4) to end of row.
Row 7: (P3, k4) to end of row.
Row 8: (K3, p4) to end of row.
Row 9: (P4, k3) to end of row.
Row 10: (K3, p4) to end of row.
Row 11: (P3, cable 4) to end of row.
Row 12: K3, (k twice into next 2 sts, k3) to end of row.
Continue in pattern for 7'' (17.5 cm) or length desired.

Armholes:
Cast off 5 sts at beginning of next 2 rows.
K2 tog at each end of every row until 59 sts remain.
Continue until armhole measures 5'' (13 cm).
Work in pattern on first 17 sts. Place next 25 sts on holder.
Work in pattern on next 17 sts until armhole measures 5½'' (14 cm). Cast off. Work other side to match.

Front

Work as for back.

Sleeves

Cast on 36 sts using 2.75 mm (12) needles.
Work in k1, p1, rib for 1'' (2.5 cm), increasing evenly 9 sts across the last row.
Change to 3.25 mm (10) needles. Work in cable as for back of jumper, increasing 1 st every 6th row until you have 56 sts. Work the extra st purl.
Cast off.

Make up

Join shoulder seams with right side facing. Pick up and knit 18 sts evenly each side of neck and sts on holder. Work in k1, p1, rib for 2'' (5 cm) or length desired. Sew side and sleeve seams. Do not press.

36: AGATHA

A vinyl walking doll 32'' (81 cm).
Doll is wearing a tweed ensemble knitted in Anny Blatt Calcutta 7-ply yarn on 4 mm (8)
needles. 7 × 50 g balls are required. The detachable collar is worked in DMC 10 Cotton on
3 mm (11) needles and 2.25 mm (13) needles at the neck edge. Five small buttons.

DRESS

Cast on 153 sts.
Knit 7 rows.
Work in st st for 10½'' (27 cm) or length desired.
Shape waist:
K1, (k2 tog) 76 times (77 sts).
Knit 5 rows.
Work 12 rows st st.
Divide for front and backs:
Row 1: K17, cast off 4 sts, k35, cast off 4 sts, k17.
Continue on last group of sts for right back.
Dec at armhole edge in alternate rows 3 times (14 sts).
Work 14 rows.
Shape shoulder:
Cast off 4 sts at beginning of next row.
Work 1 row.
Cast off.
Join yarn to next group of sts for front.
Dec at each end of alternate rows 3 times (29 sts).
Work 5 rows.
Shape neck:
K9, cast off 11 sts, k9.
Dec at neck edge in alternate rows until 4 sts remain.
Cast off.
Join yarn to remaining sts. Work other side of neck to correspond.
Join yarn to remaining group of sts for left back. Work to correspond with right back.

Sleeves

Using 3 mm (11) needles cast on 40 sts. Work in k2, p2, rib for 2'' (5 cm).
Change to 4 mm (8) needles. Work in st st until sleeve measures 4⅜'' (11 cm), ending with purl row.
Shape top of sleeve:
Cast off 2 sts at beginning of next 2 rows.
Dec at each end of next and alternate rows until 27 sts remain, then in every row until 5 sts remain.
Cast off.

Neckband

Join shoulder seams using 4 mm (8) needles. Pick up and knit 55 sts evenly around neckline.
Knit 6 rows. Cast off.

Right back band

Using 4 mm (8) needles, cast on 6 sts. Knit, making 4 buttonholes evenly along band (buttonhole k1, m1, k2 tog). Cast off. Sew to back above garter st band to neck edge.

Left back band

Work as right back band omitting buttonholes.
Sew into place.

Make up

Press work lightly, taking care not to flatten garter st. Join sleeve seams and sew in sleeves. Sew buttons onto band to correspond with buttonholes.

Collar

Using 3 mm (11) needles, cast on 105 sts and purl one row.
Row 1: K2 tog, (m1, p1, k3, p1, m1, k3 tog) to end of row, ending last repeat with k2 tog.
Row 2: P2, (k1, p3) to last 3 sts, k1, p2.
Row 3: (K2, p1, m1, k3 tog, m1, p1, k1) to last st, k1.
Row 4: As Row 2.
Repeat Rows 1–4 until work measures 2'' (5 cm).
Using 2.25 mm (13) needles, work in k1, p1, rib for ½'' (1 cm).
Cast off.

BERET

Cast on 64 sts using 4 mm (8) needles.
Work 4 rows in k1, p1, rib, then 4 rows st st.
Row 9: Inc in every 2nd st to end of row.
Row 10: Purl.
Row 11: (K10, k2 tog) to end of row.
Row 12: Purl.
Row 13: (K9, k2 tog) to end of row.
Row 14: Purl.
Continue shaping this way until you work k1, k2 tog across row.
Purl the next row.
(K2 tog) to end of row.
Next row purl.
Cut yarn and thread through remaining sts. Draw up and fasten securely. Sew neatly and press lightly.

BAG

Cast on 24 sts using 4 mm (8) needles.
Work in st st for 6'' (15 cm).
K2 tog each end of every alternate row for 4 rows.
Decrease each end of every row until 8 sts remain. Cast off. Sew up side seams. Fold over flap and fasten with press stud or button. Use chain or knitted cord for handle.

37: LUCY, RINGER & ELIZABETH

Lucy is holding a length of Victorian eyelet lace, knitted in DMC 100 Cotton Blanc on 1 mm (20) needles.

Lucy the Knitter and Ringer the Dollmaker, crafted by Ria Warke.

Reproduction doll by Thea Moore 5'' (13 cm).
Elizabeth is wearing a knitted dress designed and made by Thea in DMC 20 Cotton;
1.25 mm (18) needles.
Doll from David Moore collection.

VICTORIAN EYELET LACE

Cast on 24 sts. Knit one row.
Row 1: (K3, cast off 3 sts) twice, k6.
Row 2: K6, (m1, k3) 3 times.
Row 3: (K3, k3 in next st) twice, k6.
Row 4: Knit (24 sts).
Row 5: Cast on 3 sts, knit these 3 sts, (cast off 3 sts, k3) twice, k9.
Row 6: K9, (m1, k3) twice.
Row 7: (K3, k3 in next st) twice, k9.
Row 8: Knit (27 sts).
Row 9: Cast on 3 sts, (k3, cast off 3 sts) twice, k12.
Row 10: K12, (m1, k3) twice.
Row 11: (K3, k3 in next st) twice, k12.
Row 12: Knit (30 sts).
Row 13: Cast on 3 sts, (k3, cast off 3 sts) once, k15.
Row 14: K15, (m1, k3) twice.
Row 15: (K3, k3 in next st) twice, k15.
Row 16: Knit (33 sts).
Row 17: (Cast off 3 sts, k3) twice, cast off 3 sts, k12.
Row 18: K12, (m1, k3) twice.
Row 19: (K3, k3 in next st) twice, k12.
Row 20: Knit (30 sts).
Row 21: (Cast off 3 sts, k3) twice, cast off 3 sts, k9.
Row 22: K9, (m1, k3) twice.
Row 23: (K3, k3 in next st) twice, k9.
Row 24: Knit (27 sts).
Row 25: (Cast off 3 sts, k3) twice, cast off 3 sts, k6.
Row 26: K6, (m1, k3) twice.
Row 27: (K3, k3 in next st) twice, k6.
Row 28: Knit (24 sts).
Repeat Rows 5–28 until length desired.

N.B. 1: K3 in next st = (k1, p1, k1) in m1 of previous row.
N.B. 2: Cast off 3 sts = count the st left on needle.

ELIZABETH

Using 1.25 mm (18) needles and DMC 20 Blanc, cast on 60 sts.
Rows 1 and 2: Knit.
Row 3: (K2, p2) to end of row.
Row 4: Knit.
Repeat Rows 3–4 until 30 rows have been worked.
Row 31: (P2 tog, p2) to end of row.
Rows 32–35: St st.

Row 36: K10, cast off 2 sts, k20, cast off 2 sts, k10.
Work on last 10 sts in st st for 12 rows.
Cast off 5 sts at neck edge.
Work in st st on remaining 5 sts for 4 rows.
Cast off.
Work 12 rows st st on 20 sts at centre.
Then k5, cast off 10 sts, k5.
Work in st st on 1st 5 sts for 4 rows.
Cast off.
Repeat for other side.
Work other half of back.

Sleeves

Cast on 20 sts.
Rows 1 and 2: Knit.
Row 3: (K2, inc 1) to end of row.
Row 4: Purl.
Row 5: (K2, inc 1) to end of row.
Row 6: Purl.
Row 7: Knit.
Row 8: Purl.
Row 9: Cast off 4 sts, k to end of row.
Row 10: Cast off 4 sts, p to end of row.
Row 11: Cast off 2 sts, k to end of row.
Row 12: Cast off 2 sts, p to end of row.
Repeat Rows 11–12 twice.
Row 17: Cast off 4 sts, k to end of row.
Row 18: Cast off 4 sts, p to end of row.
Row 19: Cast off.

Collar

Work 10 repeats of Larissa Lace (see page 45).

Make up

Press work. Sew shoulders and sleeve seams. Sew back seam to waist. Insert sleeves, easing fullness.
Make a placket for dress closure:
Pick up 13 sts around back opening.
Rows 1 and 2: Knit.
Row 3: K1, (m1, k2 tog) to end of row.
Row 4: Knit.
Cast off.
Sew on tiny beads as buttons.
Sew lace around neck.

38: NECK RUFFLE

Knitted in Anny Blatt Gyps'Anny 2-ply yarn with 4 mm (8) needles. Approximately 1 × 25 g ball.

Cast on 10 sts.
Row 1: M1, k to end of row.
Rows 2–20: Repeat Row 1 until you have 30 sts.
Row 21: M1, (k2 tog) twice, k to end of row.
Repeat Row 21 19 times (10 sts).

Continue until there are 6 points on each side of the strip, or work until length desired.
Cast off.
Adjust ruffle around doll's neck. Fasten with a decorative pin.

39: BRIDGET

A knitted doll by Kathy Grin fully clothed in knitted garments. Quantities of materials in pattern.

DOLL

18'' (46 cm) doll with movable arms and legs.

Materials

100 g Champion 3-ply unbleached cotton
2 mm (14) needles
Small pieces of brown or blue, and also black, felt for eyes
Embroidery thread
Polyester fibrefill
Wig (available at doll studios)
4 flat buttons

N.B.: In this pattern
Inc 1 st = k1, p1 into 1 st
Dec 1 st = k2 tog

Front and back

Row 1: Knit.
Row 2: Purl.
Inc at each end of next and every row until there are
20 sts on needle.
Next Row: Purl.
Next Row: Inc each end of next and every 8th row (32 sts).
Work 12 rows st st.
Cast off 10 sts at beginning of next 2 rows.
Work 2 rows st st.
Inc each end of next and every alternate row (24 sts).
Work 9 rows st st.
Row 1: Dec each end of needle in next row.
Row 2: Purl.
Repeat Rows 1–2 once.
Work 2 rows st st.
Inc each end of needle in next row.
Next Row: Purl.
Repeat last 2 rows twice.
Work 8 rows st st.
Next Row: Dec each end of needle.
Purl.
Work 2 rows st st.
Dec each end of needle.
Purl.
Place marker at beginning of row to assist in row
counting.
Work 48 rows st st.
Dec each end of next and every 4th row until 12 sts
remain.
Work 3 rows st st.
Cast on 10 sts at beginning of next 2 rows.
Work 12 rows st st.

Dec each end of next and every 8th row until 20 sts
remain.
Purl.
Dec each end of next and every alternate row until 10
sts remain.
Work 3 rows st st.
Cast off.

Side piece

(Work 2, 1 in reverse)
Cast on 15 sts.
Work 12 rows st st.
Inc at end of next row (at beginning for reverse).
Work 5 rows st st.
Repeat last 6 rows twice.
Work 4 rows st st.
Dec at end of next row (at beginning for reverse).
Work 3 rows st st.
Repeat last 4 rows once.
Inc at beginning of next row (at end for reverse).
Work 3 rows st st.
Repeat last 4 rows twice.
Work 6 rows st st.
Dec at beginning of next row (at end for reverse).
Work 3 rows st st.
Repeat last 4 rows twice.
Dec at each end of next row.
Work 3 rows st st.
Dec at each end of next row.
Purl 1 row.
Cast on 3 sts at beginning of next row (at end for reverse).
Purl 1 row.
Next Row: Cast on 2 sts at beginning (at end for reverse),
inc at end (at beginning for reverse).
Purl 1 row.
Repeat last 2 rows once.
Next Row: Inc each end of needle.
Work 3 rows st st.
Next Row: Dec at beginning (at end for reverse), inc at
end (at beginning for reverse).
Purl.
Inc at end of row (at beginning for reverse).
Purl.
Next Row: Dec at beginning of row (at end for reverse),
inc at end (at beginning for reverse).
Purl.
Repeat last 2 rows once.
Inc at end of row (at beginning for reverse).
Purl.
Inc at both ends of row.
Work 3 rows st st.
Repeat last 4 rows once.

Inc at beginning (at end for reverse).
Purl.
Repeat last 2 rows once.
Work 2 rows st st.
Dec both ends of row and alternate row once.
Purl.
Cast off 3 sts at beginning of next 6 rows.
Cast off.

Legs

Cast on 21 sts.
Work 6 rows st st.
Inc in 1st and every 5th st (26 sts).
Work 9 rows st st.
Inc in 1st and every 5th st (32 sts).
Purl.
Work 44 rows st st.

Shape leg as follows:
Inc at beginning of row.
Work 3 rows st st.
Inc at end of row.
Work 3 rows st st.
Continue shaping until there are 40 sts.
Dec at beginning of row.
Work 3 rows st st.
Dec at end of row.
Work 3 rows st st.
Continue this way until there are 34 sts.
Dec at both ends of row.
Purl.
Break off yarn.
Sl 1, sl 11 sts onto a st holder, k 10 sts, sl 11 sts onto a st holder.
Work 13 rows (for instep).
Pick up 11 sts from instep, purl the 11 sts, p 11 sts from st holder.
K 32 sts, pick up 11 sts from instep, k the 11 sts, k11 sts from st holder (54 sts).
Work 11 rows st st.

Shape foot as follows:
Row 1: K2 tog, k21, sl 1, k1, psso, k4, k2 tog, k21, k2 tog.
Row 2 and every alternate row: Purl.
Row 3: K2 tog, k19, sl 1, k1, psso, k4, k2 tog, k19, k2 tog.
Row 5: K2 tog, k17, sl 1, k1, psso, k4, k2 tog, k17, k2 tog.
Row 7: K2 tog, k15, sl 1, k1, psso, k4, k2 tog, k15, k2 tog.
Row 8: Purl.
Cast off.

Arms

(Work 4, 2 in reverse.)
Cast on 6 sts.
Work 2 rows st st.
Inc at beginning of row until there are 20 sts.
Work 24 rows st st.
Next Row: Dec at both ends of row.
Purl.
Repeat last 2 rows once.
Work 2 rows st st.
Inc both ends of row.
Purl.
Work 24 rows st st.
Dec both ends of following 2 rows.
Work 2 rows st st.
Next Row: Inc at beginning of row.
Next Row: Inc at end of row.
Next Row: Inc at beginning of row.
Work 3 rows st st.
Cast off 3 sts at beginning of row, dec 1 st at end of row (thumb shaping).
Next Row: Dec at end of row.
Dec both ends of row and every alternate row until 6 sts remain.
Cast off.
Reverse thumb shaping for other side of arm.

Assembling Bridget

Lighty press work on wrong side. Sew together 2 side pieces of the body at cast on edges. Pin body pieces, matching neck and cheek seams. Sew together, leaving an opening for filling. Firmly stuff with fibrefill, especially the neck area. Sew the seam together.
Stitch around neck and waist. Fasten thread securely. Sew arm pieces together matching thumbs and elbows. Leave small space in top arm side seam for filling. Fill hands, using small plugs of filling. Outline fingers and thumb with running sts. Fill rest of arm firmly. Sew up top seam. Stitch a running st around wrist, pull to shape the wrist. Fasten off. Sew dimple in elbow.
Sew feet and back seam of legs matching shapings. Leave small opening in top seam for filling. Firmly stuff with fibrefill. Sew up seam.
Using a long needle sew arms and legs to body, using flat buttons on outside of limbs and connecting both arms and legs through body.

PANTALOONS AND PETTICOAT

Materials

2 × 50 g balls white 4-ply cotton
2 mm (14) and 2.25 mm (13) needles
white ribbon
2 small buttons

Pantaloons

Using 2 mm (14) needles, cast on 93 sts.
Row 1 (right side): K3, * sl 1, k1, psso, sl 2, k3 tog, p2sso, k2 tog, k4, repeat from * to last 12 sts, sl 1, k1, psso, sl 2, k3 tog, p2sso, k2 tog, k3.
Row 2: P4, * m1, p1, m1, p6, repeat from * to last 5 sts, m1, p1, m1, p4.
Row 3: K1, m1, * k2, sl 1, k1, psso, k1, k2 tog, k2, m1, repeat from * to last st, k1.
Row 4: P2, * m1, p2, m1, p3, m1, p2, m1, p1, repeat from * to last st, p1.
Row 5: K2, m1, k1, * m1, sl 1, k1, psso, k1, sl 1, k2 tog, psso, k1, k2 tog, (m1, k1) 3 times, repeat from * to last 12 sts, m1, sl 1, k1, psso, k1, sl 1, k2 tog, psso, k1, k2 tog, m1, k1, m1, k2.
Row 6: Purl.
Row 7: K5, m1, sl 2, k3 tog, p2sso, m1, k7, repeat from * to last 10 sts, m1, sl 2, k3 tog, p2sso, m1, k5 (73 sts).
Knit 3 rows.
Row 11: K1, (m1, k2 tog) to end of row.
Knit 3 rows.
Work 48 rows st st.
Next Row: Dec both ends of needle.
Work 3 rows st st.
Repeat last 4 rows 3 times (65 sts).
Mark beginning of row with coloured thread to assist in row counting.
Work 18 rows in st st.

Shaping:
Row 1: K12, turn.
Row 2: Sl 1, p to end of row.
Row 3: K22, turn.
Row 4: Sl 1, p to end of row.
Row 5: K32, turn.
Row 6: Sl 1, p to end of row.
Row 7: Knit.
Row 8: Purl.
Rows 9–10: K1, p1, to end of row.
Row 11: K1, * m1, k2 tog, repeat from * to end of row.

Row 12: K1, * k1, p1, repeat from * to end of row.
Work 2 rows in rib.
Cast off.
Work another piece, reverse shaping.
Press lightly on wrong side. Sew up front and back seams.
Sew leg seams, matching eyelet rows. Press seams.
Thread ribbon through holes. Thread ribbon or cord through holes at waist.

Petticoat

Cast on 119 sts.
Work 14 rows as for pantaloons (93 sts).
Work 5 rows st st.
Knit 3 rows.
Row 20: K1, (m1, k2 tog) to end of row.
Knit 3 rows.
Work in st st until work measures 6¼'' (16 cm).
Next Row: (K2 tog) to end of row (47 sts).
Next Row: K2 tog, k1, p1, k1, p2 tog, * (k1, p1) twice, k1, p2 tog, repeat from * to last 5 sts, k1, p1, k1, k2 tog (39 sts).
Change to 2 mm (14) needles.
Work 4 rows k1, p1, rib.
Change to 2.75 mm (12) needles.
Work 6 rows st st.
Cast off 2 sts at beginning of next 4 rows.
Work 7 rows st st.
Knit 3 rows.
Next Row: K1, (m1, k2 tog) to end of row.
Knit 3 rows.
Work 2 rows st st.
K12, cast off 7 sts, k12.
Purl 1 row.
Cast off 1 st at beginning of row and every alternate row until 9 sts remain.
Work 2 rows st st.
Cast off.
Work other shoulder to correspond.

Back:
Work as front (omitting garter st and eyelet rows in bodice).

Press front and back lightly on wrong side of work.
Sew side seams. Press seams.
Make small loops on front of shoulders. Sew buttons on back shoulders.
Thread ribbon through holes. Finish with dainty bow on skirt.

SKIRT AND TOP

Materials

3 balls Pinqouin Bambou or 6-ply cotton
6 buttons
piece elastic
2.75 mm (12) and 3 mm (11) needles

Skirt

Cast on 93 sts on 3 mm (11) needles.
Work 4 rows moss st.
Work in st st until work mesures 8¼ '' (21 cm).
Next Row: K1, (k2 tog) to end of row (47 sts).
Change to 2.75 mm (12) needles.
Work 3 rows k1, p1, rib.
Next Row: K1, (m1, k2 tog) to end of row.
Work 3 rows k1, p1, rib.
Cast off.

Make up:
Sew side seams. Turn over at eyelets to form hem. Sew hem. Thread through elastic to fit doll's waist and sew firmly.

Top front

Cast on 38 sts on 2.75 mm (12) needles.
Work 6 rows k1, p1, rib.
Change to 3 mm (11) needles.
Work 14 rows st st.
Cast off 2 sts at beginning of next 4 rows.
Cast off 1 st at beginning of next 2 rows (28 sts).
Work 16 rows st st.
Next Row: K11, cast off 6 sts, k11.
Purl.
Dec at beginning of neck edge twice.
Cast off.
Work other shoulder to correspond.

Top back

Cast on 18 sts on 2.75 mm (12) needles.
Work 6 rows k1, p1 rib.
Change to 3 mm (11) needles.
Work 14 rows st st.
Cast off 2 sts at beginning of next and following alternate row.
Cast off 1 st at beginning of next alternate row.

Work 22 rows in st st.
Cast off.
Knit other half to correspond.
Pick up 40 sts evenly along centre of back.
Knit 1 row.
Next Row: K2, * m1, k2 tog, k5, repeat from * to last st, k1 (6 buttonholes).
Knit 2 rows.
Cast off.
Work other half, omitting buttonholes.

Top sleeves

Cast on 28 sts using 2.75 mm (12) needles.
Work 6 rows in k1, p1, rib.
Change to 3 mm (11) needles.
Row 7: Inc in 1st and every 3rd st (38 sts).
Row 8: Purl.
Work 22 rows in st st.
Cast off 2 sts at beginning of next 4 rows.
Dec 1 st at beginning of every following row until 18 sts remain.
Cast off.

Top collar

(Work 2 pieces)
Using 3-ply cotton and 2 mm (14) needles, cast on 7 sts.
Row 1: K3, m1, k2 tog, m2, k2.
Row 2: K3, p1, k2, m1, k2 tog, k1.
Row 3: K3, m1, k2 tog, k4.
Row 4: Cast off 2 sts, k3, m1, k2 tog, k1.
Repeat Rows 1–4 10 times.
Cast off.

Make up top

Sew shoulder seams. Stitch collar pieces to neck. Sew sleeves into armholes, easing fullness at top. Sew sleeve and side seams. Sew on buttons.

SLEEVELESS JACKET

Materials

1 ball Anny Blatt Victoria (white)
1 ball Anny Blatt Victoria (contrast)
3.50 mm (9) needles

Cast on 72 sts.
Knit 2 rows in white.
Knit 2 rows contrast.
Repeat these 4 rows, working 32 rows.
Row 33: K18, leave remaining sts on holder.
Rows 34-35: Knit.
Row 36: Cast off 1 st at armhole edge, and in alternate rows.
Continue in pattern until you have worked 56 rows.
Cast off 2 sts at neck edge and in alternate rows.
Cast off 1 st at neck edge.
Knit 3 rows.
Cast off.
Pick up 18 sts from holder for left side of jacket. Work to correspond with right side. Move remaining 38 sts from holder onto needle.
Knit 2 rows.
Cast off 1 st at beginning of next 4 rows.
Work in pattern until same length as front.
Cast off.

With white yarn and right side of work facing, pick up 46 sts evenly along armhole edge.
Knit 4 rows.
Cast off.
Work other armhole the same.

Sew shoulder seams.
With white yarn and right side of work facing, pick up 29 sts from jacket front, 9 sts from neck, 12 sts from back, 9 sts from neck, 29 sts from front (88 sts).
Row 1: Knit.
Row 2: K29, k twice in next st, k28, k twice in next st, k29.
Row 3: Knit.
Row 4: K29, k twice in next st, k30, k twice in next st, k29.
Cast off.

SHOES

1 ball Anny Blatt Victoria

Using 3.5 mm (9) needles and contrasting thread, cast on 25 sts.
Knit 32 rows.
Row 33: K1, (k2 tog, k2) to end of row (19 sts).
Row 34: Knit.
Row 35: K1, (k2 tog) to end of row (13 sts).
Row 36: Knit.
Row 37: (K2 tog) 3 times, k1, (k2 tog) 3 times (7 sts).
Cast off.
Sew back seam. Sew front seam to instep, easing in toe.
Trim shoe as desired.

40: PEGGY

Peggy is wearing the cape from Pattern 7: Vilma, on page 35.
Her hat was fashioned from a length of loop knitting in Missoni Panarea. For loop knitting directions see Pattern 4: Cara Wilkie-Davey, on page 27.
The outfit shows how you can use the patterns in the book to mix and match your dolls' ensembles.

Bibliography

De Dillmont, Thèrése: *Encyclopedia of Needlework*, DMC Publication, Mullhouse, France 1924.

Klickman, Flora: *The Modern Knitting Book*, Published by The Girls' Own and Woman's Magazine, London 1914.

Lewis, Susanna E.: *Knitting Lace*, Taunton Press, USA 1992.

Mrs Leach's Fancy Work Basket, R.S. Cartwright, London 1887.

Needlecraft Practical Journals, W. Briggs & Co. Ltd, 34 Cannon Street, Manchester, *c.*1911–1930.

Rutt, Richard, The Rt Rev.: *A History of Hand Knitting*, B.T. Batsford Ltd, London 1987.

Sibbald and Souter, *Dainty Work for Busy Fingers*, S.W. Partridge & Co. Ltd, London 1915.

Thomas, Mary: *Mary Thomas's Book of Knitting Patterns*, Hodder & Stoughton Ltd, London 1985.

Weldon's Practical Knitter, series published by Weldon Ltd, The Strand, London, *c.*1890–1911.

Wright, Mary: *Cornish Guernseys and Knit Frocks*, Alison Hodges, Cornwall 1979.

Wright, Mary: *Granny's Lace Knitting and Great Granny's Lace Knitting*, self published, Cornwall 1986.

Zimmerman, Elizabeth: *Knitter's Almanac*, Dover, New York 1981.

Zimmerman, Elizabeth: *Knitting Around*, Schoolhouse Press, Pittsville, Wisconsin 1989.

Guilds

The British Knitting and Crochet Guild
Membership Secretary: Anne Budsworth
228 Chester Road North
Kidderminster
Worcestershire DY10 ITH Great Britain

The *Knitters' Guild of New South Wales Inc.*
The Guild Secretary
PO Box 70
Bexley South NSW 2207

Suppliers

The Black Sheep Gallery
Shop 3, Kingston Plaza
80 Jardine Street
Kingston ACT 2604
(06) 295 2485

Dunbar Cottage Gallery
80 Macquoid Street
Queanbeyan NSW 2620
(06) 299 4198

Queanbeyan Cottage Crafts
Millhouse Gallery
49 Collett Street
Queanbeyan NSW 2620
(06) 299 2011

The Sewing Spot
Shop 7, Crawford Centre
Crawford Street
Queanbeyan NSW 2620
(06) 297 1695

Fyshwick Antique Centre
77 Wollongong Street
Fyshwick ACT 2609
(06) 280 4541

Living in Style
Shop 4, Style Arcade
Manuka ACT 2603
(06) 295 6894

Doll and Craft Publications
Carol and Peter Chisholm
Chenka Pty Ltd
83 Wollongong Street
Fyshwick ACT 2609
(06) 280 6855

For information on heirloom
lingerie contact:
Rose White Designs
P.O. Box 13
Kippax ACT 2615
(*SAE please*)

Champion Textiles
16 O'Connell Street
Newtown NSW 2042
(02) 519 6677
(*Mail order service*)

DMC Needlecraft Pty Ltd
51–55 Carrington Road
Marrickville NSW 2204
(02) 559 3088

For information on miniature
furniture contact the craftsman:
Flick Evans
P.O. Box 59
Somers Vic. 3927

Bendigo Woollen Mills
Lansell Street
Bendigo Vic. 3550
(054) 42 4600
(*Mail order*)

Ormond Antiques
10 Ormond Parade
Hurstville NSW 2220
(02) 570 2554

Doll Studios

Blythe Bébés
61 Dundas Court
Phillip ACT
(06) 285 4276

Ria Warke, 'The Doll Works'
71 Leichhardt Street
Kingston ACT 2604
(06) 295 0697

Ellen Watt Studio
25 Graham Place
Queanbeyan NSW 2620
(06) 297 7346

Jan Clements, Dollcarver
19 High Street
Yackandandah Vic. 3749
(060) 27 1320

Kathie Savage
Cedar House
165 High Street
Berwick Vic. 3806
(03) 707 3374

Index